MODERN
Spice

INSPIRED INDIAN FLAVORS
FOR THE CONTEMPORARY KITCHEN

Monica Bhide

FOREWORD BY MARK BITTMAN

SIMON & SCHUSTER

New York   London   Toronto   Sydney

Simon & Schuster
1230 Avenue of the Americas
New York, NY 10020

First Simon & Schuster hardcover edition April 2009

The essay "Counting Peas" was previously published in *The Washington Post,* and the essay "What
Is Real Cooking?" appeared on the website SauteWednesday, www.sautewednesday.com.

SIMON & SCHUSTER and colophon are registered trademarks
of Simon & Schuster, Inc.

For information about special discounts for bulk purchases,
please contact Simon & Schuster Special Sales at
1-800-456-6798 or business@simonandschuster.com.

Designed by Jaime Putorti
Modern Spice Bowl illustration by Jason Snyder

Manufactured in the United States of America

10   9   8   7   6   5   4   3   2   1

Library of Congress Cataloging-in-Publication Data
Bhide, Monica.
    Modern Spice : inspired Indian flavors for the contemporary kitchen / by Monica Bhide.
        p. cm.
        1. Cookery, Indian. 2. Cookery, American. I. Title.

TX724.5.I4 B553 2009   641.5954 dc—22
                                                             2008047281

ISBN-13: 978-1-5011-0087-1
ISBN-10:   1-5011-0087-4

To the four amazing men in my life—

MY BOYS, JAI AND ARJUN,

MY LOVING HUSBAND, SAMEER,

AND MY WONDERFUL FATHER, D. N. SAIGAL

ACKNOWLEDGMENTS

They say it takes a village to raise a child. I say the same about writing books. In this case, however, my village is an e-village. Friends, family, mentors, guides, colleagues, chefs, writing buddies, testers, and tasters from all over the world have helped shape this book.

I would like to thank Janet and Jim Walters, Anna Nielson, Barbara Hiel, Gingerlly, Apolina Fos, Bharat Josiam, Shubhangi Ambedekar, S. Sudha, Suman Vardarajan, Denise Schipani, Andrea King Collier, Randy Hecht, Melina Kendrick Tye, Lisa Armstrong, Eman and Rami Safadi, Ashok Bajaj, Vinu and Aradhana Luthra, Shirley and Hersh Taur, Heather Freeman, Jeanie and Jim Thomas, Amber Pfau, Michele Sewell, Ya-Roo Yang, Suzanne Fass, Gwen Moran, Emily Kaiser, Susan Koch, Kedar and Vrinda Deval, Anil and Maya Nair, Vikram Sunderam, Makrand and Meghana Bhave, Dimple and Vishal Agarwal, Jennifer Haupt, Suzanne Arthur, Alyona and Sanjeev Kapoor, K. N. Vinod, Sudhir Seth, José Andrés, Mike and Sayli Moskowitz, Shree and Smita Gondhalekar, Kristin Ohlson, Diane Morgan, Melissa McCart, Amanda McClements, Ellen Shapiro and Steven Shaw, Nycci Nellis, Don Rockwell, Candy Sagon, Tom Sietsema, David Leite, Rachel Weingarten, Rebecca Pawlowski, and Raghavan Iyer.

To my darling family: my parents, D. N. and Sneh Saigal; my in-laws, B. M. and Shashi Bhide; my sister, Arti, and her hubby, Sumir Bahl; my aunt Kanta Saigal; and my boys, Arjun and Jai Bhide. I owe my sanity to my husband, Sameer Bhide.

There is another saying—when the student is ready, the teacher appears. In my case, my writing career would not have even been possible without the support, encouragement, and generosity of souls like Mark Bittman, Paula Wolfert, Toni Allegra, Jeanne McManus, Judy Weinraub, Julie Sahni, Sacha Cohen, Gabi Redford, Frances Largeman Roth, and my book editor Sydny Miner for believing in my voice.

Finally, I want to thank Michael Psaltis, my agent, for believing in my writing and for putting up with me for all these years!

CONTENTS

FOREWORD

It's an understatement, and probably even a cliché, but here in North America, Indian cooking remains the most underrated and probably least understood of the world's great cuisines. Though we have thankfully progressed from the days when I learned how to cook, when to get beyond curry you really had to do some digging, we're still a ways from seeing Indian food as we do Italian. Yet the cooking of this gigantic subcontinent is as varied and intriguing as that of the boot-shaped peninsula in the Mediterranean.

It's not an exaggeration to say that there is not a cuisine that uses spices with more grace and craft than that of India. Really, what we outsiders think of as Indian cuisine is actually a vast collection of cuisines, because the national borders encompass literally hundreds of ethnicities. And it's even more complicated than that, since the cuisine we call Indian crosses national borders. (But maybe that's a political discussion.)

The problem Americans have long had in making Indian food at home has been inaccessibility, and over the course of the last generation we have begun to see that change as increasing numbers of non-Indian home cooks have discovered its joys and found the resources. And those resources have been thankfully increased by the presence of Monica

Bhide, and especially the introduction of the long-awaited *Modern Spice*.

In many ways, Monica is perfectly suited to this challenge: she was born in New Delhi, but has lived in the northeastern United States for most of her adult life. She has a formal education in engineering which, given that this has nothing to do with cooking, is all the better when it comes to educating home cooks. As she says, the Indian-American cooks of her generation "love tradition but embody change. Just like traditional dishes cooked with painstaking effort reflect our mother's and grandmother's generations, our dishes reflect our modern lifestyles. They are easy, fun, and intensely flavorful."

It's true. I have known Monica only since food, cooking, and teaching the wonders of Indian cooking became her guiding passion, and she has gone at it with a dedication I haven't seen in many others so that she could make her recipes, her teaching, her books "easy, fun, and intensely flavorful." She has set about to learn as much as she could, primarily but not exclusively about Indian cooking. If it took traveling, she did it. If it required challenging assignments, she tackled them. If it required chasing down someone she thought she could learn from—well, she chased.

Monica is someone who can think, cook, teach, taste, and write—it's a good combination and it's all on display here. Her essays, tangential bonuses, will ensnare you (check out the touching one preceeding the ginger tea recipe). Her recipes will entice you. My favorites so far are: potato-peanut tikkis (these are unbelievable); stir-fried lamb, which could easily become routine—but tastes so great; and shrimp in green mango butter, a surprising combination that will, I hope, become less surprising as the years go by. But it won't be less delicious, and that's the point.

MARK BITTMAN

MODERN Spice

MODERN SPICE

. . . .

A husband says to his wife, "Honey, I love the way you bake ham. But why do you cut the end off? That is my most favorite part."
"My mother cooks it this way," she replies. "It's tradition."
Later she calls her mother. "Mom, why do we cut the end off the ham?"
The mother does not know. She calls her mother-in-law, from whom she learned the recipe.
"Why do we cut the ends off, Mama?"
"Ah, that," says the 100-year-old mother-in-law. "When I first cooked a ham, I didn't have a pan big enough."

I love this story—just because we have always done things in one way, it does not make it the only way to do something. So if fennel- and-chile-crusted tilapia and basmati rice with pine nuts and mint, accompanied by a Guava Bellini, does not sound Indian to you, think again! Indian food has come a long way from the same old, same old world of mango lassis and tandoori chicken. While traditional Indian cooking required slaving in the kitchen for hours, modern Indian cooking makes a virtue of quick-cook techniques. While traditional Indian cooking relied on a myriad of spices and herbs, modern Indian cooking focuses on taking a few spices and bringing out their flavors. While traditional Indian cooking was perceived to be difficult and fussy, the foundation of modern Indian cooking is perfection in simplicity.

Yes, as a new generation of modern Indians, we are changing everything.

We love tradition, but embody change.

We respect technique, but are playful.

Our style is refined; our tastes are global.

Our new cuisine is a reflection of our lives today, here and now. Just as traditional curries and dishes cooked painstakingly from scratch reflect our mothers' and grandmothers' generations, our dishes reflect our modern lifestyles. They are easy, fun, and intensely flavorful.

This fun, sassy approach to Indian-inspired food is what you will find in this book. The recipes I have created and present here are vibrant and enticing, yet they are simple, refined, and adapted to modern lifestyles: this is Indian food as it is cooked now. This is a book for today's generation that does not want yesterday's style of doing things. As a community we are creating new styles, new traditions, and a new cuisine that needs to be captured.

This book takes Indian cooking and translates it for our generation——this book embraces the intense, spicy, Indian flavors but is not stuck on an artificial standard of authenticity that no longer exists even in India.

I understand the soul of Indian cuisine; I understand the dishes, their roots, and the richness of history that surrounds the food. It is this knowledge that sets me free and gives me the freedom to play with them, to evolve the dishes. Growing up in the Middle East, I learned authentic Indian dishes from the talented and knowledgeable hands of my father and mother. During frequent visits to India, I moved from my grandmother's kitchen to those of my mother's cousins and friends, along the way gathering delightful anecdotes and learning authentic recipes. Fifteen years ago I moved to the United States, and since then the Indian cooking that I learned has changed so much. All these experiences are what I am sharing with you in *Modern Spice*.

This book does not have any recipes for mango lassi—there are 200 books out there (including two of my own!) that you can read for that—instead it brings you a Guava Bellini. It doesn't offer chicken tikka masala; it provides a recipe for chicken gently simmered in fresh cilantro and mint. This is Indian, my way: a reflection of the Indian cooking of today and the style of the modern Indian.

Is *Modern Spice* Fusion? Authentic? Traditional?

The recipes in *Modern Spice* are not traditional Indian recipes, although they have roots in tradition and are inspired by tradition. As far as being authentic Indian—I am an authentic Indian, I am using authentic Indian spices and authentic Indian techniques. Does that make the recipes authentic Indian? Of course, I am only half joking. I strongly believe—more so each day—that authenticity is a state of mind. It is very hard to find "authentic" recipes, as the definition of authentic is different from state to state, city to city, and even household to household. The way my mother made "authentic lentils" is very different from the way my mother-in-law makes "authentic lentils" or the way my friends make them. Please keep in mind as you read and cook from this book that we are always influenced by the environment we live in. I have lived in the United States for a long time now and that is reflected in a few of the dishes—I use brussels sprouts, leeks, and even pre-made pizza crust. But I have stayed true to my spices and to my love of Indian tastes and flavors, and I am sure you will experience that as you cook the dishes in this book.

in search of authenticity—
LOCAL IS AS LOCAL DOES

· ·

"East or west, Dubai is best," my mother would tell me when I was a child. A city endowed with the luxuries of the West and blessed with the conveniences of the East, Dubai sounded like nirvana. I am Indian by birth, and have spent the past seventeen years in the United States but was raised on the tiny Islamic island of Bahrain, Dubai's less grand neighbor in the Arabian Gulf. My father traveled frequently, and Dubai was his favorite destination. "It is a city of dreams—gold lines the sidewalks," he would beam. He would always return home with a raffle ticket from the airport. "Dubai Duty-Free is raffling a Lexus. They will sell only one thousand tickets!" he'd exclaim.

One element, though, was always missing in my parents' praise of Dubai—the food. Ours was a food-obsessed household—in addition to classic Indian dishes, my father would prepare food he enjoyed on his trips—Lebanese hommous and *shis tawook* (charcoal grilled chicken), Bahraini biryanis (rice and meat casseroles), Turkish coffee, and even English fish and chips. Oddly enough Dubai's cuisine was never mentioned. I never gave it a second thought until I started writing about food for a living. "Dad, what did you eat in Dubai?" I

5

asked him. "Well, a bit of this and a bit of that," he replied. When pressed he really couldn't think of one local Dubai restaurant.

So I decide to visit Dubai, with my husband and son in tow, to discover the culinary side of the emirate. After all, what reflects a city's culture, people, and tradition better than its local cuisine?

Upon arrival at Dubai International Airport I see hordes of people in Western clothes, with a smattering in traditional black *abayas* (gowns worn by women) and white *dishdashes* (gowns worn by men). Columns topped with golden fronds, extravagant stores, and lounges line the corridors of the airport. I hear Arabic from the speakers. It will be the last time I hear that much Arabic on my trip: roughly 85 percent of Dubai's one-million-plus population is non-Emirati. The majority of the people I see appear to be of South Asian descent.

In the taxi en route to the hotel, a cool January breeze and omnipresent construction greet me. The cab zips along the glittering, skyscraper-lined Sheikh Zayed Road, Dubai's main artery joining Sharjah and Abu Dhabi. Our driver stops at a light, unable to make a left. "I could have sworn there was a turn here," he says. "They are changing the city so fast."

I witness a city being clothed in concrete. Billboards everywhere boast of a city preparing to make history with the world's tallest skyscraper, the world's largest mall, the largest theme park, even an underground luxury hotel to be connected by submarines: Vegas and Disney in one. This seemingly chaotic growth isn't random; the ruling sheikh thinks long term. I am fascinated with the sight of ladies in abayas walking alongside shorts-clad nonlocal women—in the heart of Dubai, in plain view. This is not the conservative Middle East with idyllic, quiet beaches I remember growing up in.

I arrive at the Le Meridian Mina Siyahi, opposite Dubai Media City and Dubai Internet City, passing offices of CNN and Reuters on the way. Tired and hungry after a long flight, I scan the menus at the hotel restaurants but find little Arabic food. I decide to eat at Tang, which offers French cuisine with Japanese flavors. I dine on teppanyaki chicken with searing red chile and an unusual side of sweet cherries and wild woodsy mushrooms.

The next morning, I begin my mission to find local food. I am eager to find *harees* (crushed wheat and meat) and *makbus* (meat and rice casserole) prepared to be consumed in a communal fashion. I have scoured tourist guides, talked to friends in Dubai, and located a single Emirati-style restaurant, Local House Restaurant. The menu, I find, is sparse, listing a few rice and meat dishes—which the server tells me are not available that day. I am disappointed, but the trip has just begun. I order Turkish coffee and a plate of dates. I go to the Dubai Museum next door; it's housed in an eighteenth-century fort.

Hunger pangs begin; I enter at random a store outside the museum and ask for places serving local foods. I am given the address of Ravi, in the nearby Bastakiya neighborhood, famous for old buildings with *barjeels* (wind towers that offer natural air-conditioning). I devour lunch: fried mutton chops, spicy chicken curry, garlic-infused lentils, and fresh watermelon juice. The food is flavorful and satisfying; it is South Asian.

Driving around the city I notice Starbucks Coffee, Pizza Hut, Dubai fried chicken, various Lebanese, Moroccan, Indian, Thai, Chinese, Japanese, Polynesian, and French coffee shops and restaurants.

Even if I cannot find Emirati food in the city, I am sure I can find it in the desert.

That evening I leave Dubai and head to Al Maha, a desert resort in the Dubai conservation area. A single star shines in the eerily dark sky as our rented Camry navigates toward the resort. Our driver panics, "The Camry won't make it over the dunes," he mutters. I roll down my window to get over the motion sickness and smell the resort, burning frankincense, even before I see its lights glittering quietly in the night. Our hosts—Moroccan, not Emirati as I had expected—escort us to our private villa over a path lit with tiny oil lamps, as cream-colored, spear-horned Arabian oryx (antelope) wander around us. I spot a shy honey-skinned gazelle hiding behind a small shrub. The villas, with soft curving tent-like roofs and private infinity pools, are reminiscent of a Bedouin encampment near an oasis except that the rooms include Bulgari shampoos, cable TV, mini-bars, and even an easel with a canvas for guests to capture the spirit of the desert in paint.

An eclectic pre-set dinner menu featuring an eggplant *moutabel* dip, veal, and risotto graces our table in a quaint dining hall. Over our heads, a garlic bulb-shaped chandelier twinkles. There is strudel for dessert and then a *"Tsch-euss,* goodnight" from the Sri Lankan wait staff. Obviously there are a lot of German guests here.

A chirping white-cheeked bulbul wakes me up the next morning. Today I will observe the traditional Arab art of falconry. The morning is chilly as our South African field guide drives us in his GMC truck past exotic yellow Indian flower bushes into the desert. The guides stop about a half a mile from the villas, set up the activity, and then set up a drink stand. I am expecting *kahwah,* Arab tea that was being served at the resort, simmered with cardamom and saffron. I am handed a sweet and thick hot chocolate.

The show begins as a young falcon, just six weeks in training, swoops and swerves at the orders of her trainers to catch a lure as if it were prey. "We got her from Customs," they tell us. "It is a Pakistani falcon someone was trying to smuggle in." The cold sky now surrenders to a honey sun. These sights, the people, the flowers, the falcon, the food, seem so unfamiliar, so foreign to the land.

Next I embark on a *dhow* (boat) tour of Dubai Creek, an inland waterway about 10 kilometers long and a central divider of the city. Our German-speaking Croatian guide provides commentary. *Abras* (water taxis) shuttle Dubai residents across the creek for under a few cents. Fusion cuisine takes on a new meaning here—the dinner buffet is filled with Lebanese baba ganoush, Western roasted leg of lamb, and Indian chicken tikka masala. I spot Umm Ali, Emirati bread pudding, for dessert. Warm Indian bread, naan, is being prepared in a tandoor installed on the rooftop of the *dhow.* Still no local flavors.

Perhaps the Burj Al Arab, Dubai's answer to the Eiffel Tower, will quench my quest, I think. This billowing-sail-shaped hotel, on its own private island jutting into the Arabian Sea, prides itself as the "Most Luxurious Hotel in the World." At 321 meters, the Burj is a touch taller than the Eiffel Tower.

We enter a lobby that has been called ostentatious and cheesy: a large waterfall in the center of the hall is flanked by aquariums housing over fifty species of fish. The main level boasts outsize columns plated with 24-carat gold leaf. Vibrant splashes of blue, red, and gold are everywhere. My young son, his big brown eyes open in wonderment, says, "Mamma, this looks like Aladdin's Agrabah."

The staff greets us with legendary Arabic hospitality: bateel dates to sweeten our palette, fresh towels moist with rose water to refresh our faces, and *bakhoor* (incense) to enliven our spirits. Our personal butler awaits us at our duplex. We find every conceivable amenity: a wireless laptop, multiple mini-bars, pillow menus, a butler's pantry, marbled bathrooms filled with a half-dozen large bottles of Hermès perfumes. My husband turns on one of the large plasma TVs to watch cricket. The game is quickly interrupted when the doorbell rings: the screen switches to show the guest at the door. The floor manager has come to check us in. The butler presses a button on a keypad to open the door, then another to open the drapes. A dramatic panorama of the sea opens up revealing the palm tree-shaped "Palm Jumeriah" and globe-shaped "The World"—both man-made islands being built to house shops, villas, and restaurants.

I scan the menus of their various restaurants. They offer many choices, even a Middle Eastern buffet, but not what I am looking for. I throw up my hands in despair; where is the Emirati food? Then I do what any discouraged, self-respecting writer would do. I call my father. "I am so frustrated Dad," I whine on one of my suite's ten phones. "I am having a hard time finding local foods. It's like 'there is no there there.'" "You are an engineer . . . think like one," replies Dad, reminding me of my former career. "Is your assumption faulty? Does food define a culture or does a culture define food?" I instantly recall an old lesson—to assume often makes an ass out of you and me.

Pondering this development, I leave my room and take a three-minute simulated submarine ride that takes me "into the depths of the ocean" to the Al Mahara seafood restaurant for lunch. The submarine turns out to be a cleverly disguised elevator. Admiring the dining room, surrounded by an exotic aquarium, I order from an intriguing "water menu" offering twenty-five varieties of water: from an Austrian Chantes to a Vichy Celestins from

France. I ask to see the executive chef, hoping he can guide me in my quest. Chef Jean Paul Naquin, a tall and gentle Frenchman, smiles at my question. "The closest food to 'local' here is Lebanese. Emirati food never evolved enough to be part of the culinary scene." Now I understand. After all, where do I send people when they ask me for an authentic taste of New York? Katz's Deli, a great Jewish deli, or a great pizza place. In this city of foreigners, I need to change my definition of local.

The next morning, armed with my new paradigm, I head to the upscale Egyptian-themed Wafi City mall, ornamented with concrete pharaohs and stained glass ceilings. Sitting on the terrace at the Lebanese restaurant, Wafi Gourmet, I choose a fresh mango juice, a delightful *makdous* (eggplant and walnuts in olive oil) and fresh bread from their *saj*, a Lebanese-style oven. Nougats, olives, stuffed dates, bakhlava, spices, and kebabs line the store. Happy with my "local" find I wander over to Elements, a café selling beautiful oil paintings by Iraqi painters. A light-haired gentleman smoking a *shisha* (tobacco pipe), eating sushi, and working on his laptop while seated on large pillows on the balcony of the cafe waves hello.

My destination for dinner that night is Al Nafoorah, a much-loved Lebanese restaurant at the Jumeriah Emirates Towers. Delicate lamb kebbeh, savory *fatayer* encasing spinach and onions, crisp parcels of Akawi cheese in phyllo dough, and a dish of moist chicken livers in pomegranate sauce compete to be my top food choice for the trip. Our server notices my enthusiasm. "You cannot come to a Lebanese restaurant and not try the hommous," he says. I am a harsh judge of hommous, and theirs is one of the best I have ever eaten: smooth as butter and unpretentious in flavor.

We leave the Burj, where we have been staying with my husband's college friend and his family, who have recently relocated here from Westchester County in New York. I want to get a sense of the expatriate lifestyle—no income tax and economical maid service. In contrast to their small New York apartment, the suburbs where they live are lined with airy, ornate, terraced villas surrounded by ten-foot-high walls.

The first morning here, the Azaan of Fajr, the Muslim call to early morning prayer, from a nearby mosque, jolts me out of bed at 5:30. The sound I grew up with in Bahrain for fifteen years finally makes this place seem familiar. An American citizen and a Hindu, I find home in Muslim prayer.

I walk around the neighborhood in Jumeriah searching for one of my most favorite childhood foods. In Bahrain's suburbs, Iranian bakers had set up small shops that housed ovens where they baked fresh breads or the *khubz*. I don't find any such thing in this ritzy Dubai suburb. I lament to my friends. "We buy our bread at Spinneys," they say simply. They take me to the British grocery store. I drink my cool *laban* (yogurt drink) and contemplate what the camel's milk displayed on the shelf tastes like. I follow my hosts to the wholesale fruit market: Iranian kiwis, Indonesian mangosteens, Turkish oranges, Ras-Al-Khaimah's dates. They want to purchase cardamom next, so we go to the spice souk in Deira, located off the Dubai Creek. Dhows bringing in shipments from around the Middle East crowd the waterway. The air melds aromas of cardamom, cloves, saffron, incense. I haggle with an Iranian shopkeeper over Yemeni coffee beans. He finally relents on the price and then, much to my surprise, offers free chocolates for my son. He then offers to sell me a beautiful whole saffron flower in a bottle. "You are Hindi (Indian)?" he says. "Iranian and Hindi are like brothers, I give you a good rate." A European tourist saunters in behind me and the shopkeeper's attention shifts. "You are French? French and Iranian like brothers. I give you good deal on natural Viagra."

Later that day I tell my hosts about my quest for local foods. "There is one place," they say, "where you can still find foods of Arabia—Global Village." We head to this annual shopping, carnival, and food extravaganza with pavilions of world cities. We enter "Egypt" and I am instantly drawn to the *fatir*, a bread-based dessert. The cook flings the bread in the air like pizza dough and then bakes it. He layers it with cream cheese, drizzles it with honey, and then hands it to me. We greedily eat the warm bread, the flavor of sweet honey beautifully carried by the fat in the savory cheese. We sample honey in "Yemen." Shopkeepers, in broken English, tell us about the benefits of mountain flower honey versus lowland flower honey. From what I understand, the honey cures everything from infidelity to infertility. In addition to Arabic foods and spices, I finally see a sea of locals in *abayas* and *dishdashes*.

My last night in Dubai is spent at a place picked by our friends as one of the best local places, the very chic Teatro. I am served spicy tuna sushi alongside tandoori hammour, a local fish. I look around and smile—I am surrounded, as I have been for most of the trip, by Brits, Australians, South Africans, South Asians, and yes, Arabs.

It occurs to me that nothing about the flavors of the food I have eaten on the trip have been subtle. It is as if they are competing with the burgeoning city to get the upper hand, to see who makes it to excellence first. My days here have been filled with Lebanese buffets, Movenpick ice-cream runs, lounging in Irish pubs and jazz bars, eating Japanese, Thai, Moroccan, Pan-Asian—Dubai now seems like more than just Vegas and Disney. It is a true melting pot of cultures and cuisines—an emerging New York. On steroids.

At the airport the next morning, I spot something familiar at the duty-free counter. I purchase a raffle ticket to win a BMW 7 series, one of only 1,000 tickets sold. This city of dreams has added another dreamer to its growing list.

THE MODERN
SPICE PANTRY

There are a lot of myths surrounding Indian cooking—that it's difficult and time consuming for example—but the biggest myth of all has to be that urban, middle-class Indians—in the United States or in India—don't use any packaged spices and pastes, preferring to spend hours in the kitchen grinding and mixing.

There: I said it. Feel free to be shocked.

While I exaggerate for effect, the truth is that many young Indian home cooks and even some chefs do use some packaged spice mixes like chaat masala or sambar masala. There are some spice mixes that I would *never* buy—I grind garam masala at home and would never consider buying it. But there are others, like tandoori masala and sambar powder that I not only buy but recommend to my friends, students, and family all the time. Indian cooking is all about alluring spices and flavors reflective of the diverse Indian landscape and peoples. While it is rewarding to create your own spice mixes, fresh homemade cheese, and chutneys, it does require time and patience. One has to find the right balance between authentic flavor and effort.

There used to be a time when finding Indian spices in the United States was a difficult, time-consuming, often fruitless activity. That is not the case today. Quality spices are easily available at Indian groceries, regular grocery stores, specialty spice stores, and of course on the Internet. A modest example: *paneer*, Indian cheese, is not only available at all Indian grocery stores, but is now even made in Wisconsin and being promoted by the Wisconsin Milk Marketing Board.

It is my belief that to be able to cook Indian food (or just about any other cuisine) really well, one simply needs to understand the secrets of the spices— touch them, smell them, taste them. Once you've mastered spices, you'll be able to take on just about any recipe. It is sort of like Julie Andrews in *The Sound of Music:* "When you know the notes to sing, you can sing most anything."

Mail order sources for Indian ingredients and other ingredients used in this book:

1. www.grocerybabu.com is a good source for Indian ingredients.

2. www.myonlinegroceries.com carries several brands of pickles including Ruchi.

3. Fillo Factory products are available at local grocery stores. Find a store near you at www.fillofactory.com.

4. Mochiko Sweet Rice Flour is available in most Asian grocery stores. You can find it online at www.quickspice.com.

5. Adriatic Fig Spread is available at Whole Foods supermarkets.

The Insider's Guide to the *Modern Spice* Pantry

Here is an insider's guide to time- and labor-saving Indian ingredients, so you can make a Monday night meal without too much fuss or effort.

BASIC DRY SPICE MIXES

The word *masala* simply means spice mix. It can be a dry mix or a wet mix. Spice mixes are used in Indian cooking to provide layers of flavors. There are a few basic spice mixes that are the building blocks of Indian cooking. Generally, they exemplify the cooking of the regions in India from which they originate. There has been considerable improvement over the past few years in the quality of packaged spice mixes on the market. Here are some of the more commonly used mixes.

TANDOORI MASALA:

Tandoors are large clay ovens used to roast meats and vegetables and to bake breads. Meats cooked in the tandoor stay moist on the inside while developing a distinguishing crust on the outside. Tandoors burn charcoal and cook foods at a very high temperature. (Small, portable, home-use tandoors are now available in the United States, but you can use a conventional oven or charcoal grill for most tandoori recipes.) The key to tandoori cooking is in the marination, and tandoori masala is a spice mix used in these marinades.

Tandoori foods were thought to have obtained a red color from cooking in red brick tandoors, but it's actually just food coloring. Some of the spice mixes attempt to emulate the look by adding red food coloring to their ingredients.

Brands: MDH's Tandoori Barbeque Masala or Shan's Tandoori Chicken and BBQ Mix are both excellent. The flavors are strong and clean. Shan's Tandoori Chicken and BBQ Mix is composed of red chile, ginger, nutmeg, black pepper, cardamom, cumin, mace, dried garlic, cinnamon, and aniseed. Param-Para sells a wet Tandoor Chicken Mix with an interesting note on the packet that says all the ingredients are purely vegetarian!

How to use it: Combine the spice mix with yogurt, lemon juice, ginger-garlic paste, and a bit of vegetable oil to create a perfect marinade for chicken, shrimp, tofu, or fish. Yogurt is used as a meat and poultry tenderizer in Indian cooking, and is an integral part of most tandoori marinades. You can also use the same marinade for potatoes, cauliflower, mushrooms, onions, bell peppers, and *paneer* (Indian cheese).

Sambar Powder:

A classic southern Indian spice powder used to prepare the split-yellow-lentil-based dish, sambar. Orange-hued sambar powders are a cornucopia of flavors and fragrance. Sambars are served alongside Indian *dosas* (crepes) and *idlis* (steamed fermented lentil and rice cakes), and with steaming white rice for a complete meal.

Brands: Listing its ingredients as coriander, cumin, rice, chile, fenugreek, cinnamon, and curry leaves, MTR's sambar powder is hands-down the best one on the market today. MTR makes a sambar paste and an instant sambar mix that are also convenient to use.

How to use it: The base legume used to prepare a sambar is *toor dal* (pigeon peas). The dal is cooked and set aside. Vegetables are boiled in a separate pot. The powder is then added to the cooked vegetables along with the prepared dal, tamarind, and lemon juice. Mix well and serve hot. This powder does pack a fiery punch, so add a little bit at a time until you are happy with the heat it provides.

Chaat Masala:

This classic North Indian spice mix is used as a garnish to add a final flavoring to dishes like fritters, salads, kebabs, and many street foods. It includes spices such as dried mango powder, black salt, and many more.

Brands: The best ones are MDH and Shan.

How to use it: A little goes a long way with this mix so just sprinkle a touch of it—try it on French fries, onion rings, a ripe cut papaya, or a diced boiled potato, and then sprinkle on a little lemon juice.

Curry Powders:

Believe it or not, there is no such thing as a generic curry powder in the traditional Indian kitchen. The product "curry powder" was created by the British, who ruled India many years ago, to imitate and re-create Indian flavors when they returned home. Curry powder is simply a mixture of spices. Each region in India has its own special mixes that are blended together to form "curries" or sauces. The spices used vary from manufacturer to manufacturer. Curry powders are not about heat, they are about aroma and flavor. They add sweetness, bitterness, heat, sourness, and even color to dishes. While most traditional Indian home cooks and chefs prefer to grind their own spices to create curries, specific curry powders such as chicken curry masala, vindaloo masala, and dal masala (lentil curry powder) are beginning to find a home in the Indian kitchen both here in the United States and in India. In ethnic and chain grocery stores today, you will find a wide variety of curry powders sold in cardboard boxes or small tins. Experiment with them until you find a taste that you like. My rule of thumb is always to add a couple of teaspoons (for a dish that provides four servings) and then add more if you prefer a stronger taste. Commercial curry powders tend to be stronger in their turmeric content.

Brands: My personal favorite brands are MDH, Shan, and McCormick Gourmet Collection Hot Madras Curry Powder.

How to use it: Most commercially available powders are added during the cooking stages and not as a garnish. Shan usually provides fairly good suggestions on the back of the box on how to use its spice mixes.

PAANCH PHORON:

This is a typical Eastern Indian spice mix containing five different whole spices—black mustard seeds, onion seeds, cumin seeds, fennel seeds, and fenugreek seeds. It is available at Indian grocery stores. It is typically added to hot oil to allow the spices to release their flavors and aromas.

To Store Dried Spice Mixes:

Most spice mixes are sold in cardboard boxes or in small containers. Transfer them to airtight jars and store them away from direct heat or sunlight. Try not to store your spices right next to the stove, as this will cause the spices to lose their potency. Never use a wet spoon to remove spices from a jar. To determine if a spice mix is fresh and usable, just use your nose. If it has little or no aroma, the spices have lost their effectiveness and shouldn't be used.

PANTRY

GINGER-GARLIC PASTE:

Ginger and garlic together form a layer of strong flavors upon which many North Indian curries are built. The paste also acts as a thickening agent. Preparing ginger-garlic paste from scratch is a tedious process. But while a bit less aromatic than the freshly prepared pastes, store-bought ginger-garlic paste works fine for most recipes.

Brands: SWAD, Maya, and Nirav all sell the paste in jars from 7 to 14 ounces. Salt and oil are used to preserve the paste.

How to use it: Sauté pureed ginger and garlic along with onions at the beginning of the cooking process in most Indian curries. Ginger-garlic paste cooks quickly and can burn, so watch it carefully when you cook with it. Add a tablespoon to your marinades to build flavor.

To store: Refrigerate the opened jar of paste for up to 6 weeks. You can also freeze it in an ice cube tray and use a cube as needed. The frozen paste keeps for up to 3 months. If you freeze it, place the cubes in a heavy-duty plastic bag and seal the bag well. This will ensure that the paste's powerful aroma does not permeate everything in your freezer.

MASALA CHAI SPICE TEA:

Spice tea is the quintessentially Indian drink! Cloves, ginger, cinnamon, cardamom, and even fennel are added to black tea for fragrance and flavor. While freshly prepared spice tea is still the best, some prepared teabags provide serious competition.

Brands: Sapat's Fantasy Masala Chai is marvelous. Each tea bag is perfumed with cinnamon, cloves, and cardamom.

How to use it: Brew as you would regular teabags, and add milk and sugar to taste. Don't forget to take time to smell the aroma while sipping this fragrant tea.

To store: Store in a cool place. Make sure you close the container tightly after each use to seal in the flavors.

Coconut Milk:

Traditionally, the meat of fresh coconuts is used to prepare coconut milk; it is a time-consuming process. Several companies now sell prepared coconut milk that is excellent. It is used in curries, sides, desserts, and even in drinks. Coconut milk has no lactose (obviously!). Coconut water, a clear liquid found in tender coconuts, is not a substitute for coconut milk.

Brands: A Taste of Thai makes an excellent coconut milk. It also has a thinner, "lite" version.

How to use it: Simmer meats in it, use it in desserts, or add to drinks.

To store: Refrigerate any leftovers immediately in a covered container. Use within a week.

Rooh Afza (Rose syrup):

A lovely, deep magenta sweet syrup made from flower and fruit extracts that is used to flavor water, milk, and desserts.

Brands: Only one: Hamdard. And there is *no* subsitute!

How to use it: Use as a flavoring syrup. It is very fragrant and very sweet, so start with a tablespoon per eight ounces of water and add more as needed.

To store: Store in a cool place. Make sure you close the container tightly after each use to seal in the flavors.

Basmati Rice:

The Indians' love of rice is legendary. Basmati rice in itself is a pleasure to eat—nutty, fragrant, and simply delicious. While white basmati rice (and jasmine rice, among others) has dominated the Indian rice scene, these days brown basmati is making inroads here in the United States. It is one brown rice that I have found actually does taste like rice. It plays well with spices and meats, too.

Brands: Kohinoor sells white and brown basmati rice and has just started selling wild rice. Tilda has a fantastic white basmati rice.

How to use it: Basmati rice works well in the rice cooker. However, my two cents are that cooking it in the rice cooker takes away the opportunity for you to play with your rice! Cooking it on the stove provides great opportunities to add spices, vegetables, meats, poultry—whatever your heart desires. The ratio for water to rice for cooking plain rice, on a stovetop, is one cup rice to two cups water. Rinse the rice well before use—this helps remove any contaminants and also surface starch. I don't soak my rice, but it is said to reduce cooking time and you can do so if you like. Also, my most important advice is that rice cooks best when it is left alone. Don't open the lid when it is cooking to peak inside; this allows all the wonderful steam to escape and increases cooking time. Place the rice in a pot, add the water, bring to a boil, reduce the heat to low, and cover. Cook for 15 to 20 minutes *untouched.* Then remove the lid and see where you are. If there are small craters on top of the rice and all the moisture is gone, it is done. Fluff with a fork and eat away!

To store: Store uncooked rice in a cool place. Make sure you close the container tightly after each use to seal in the flavor. You can store cooked rice, covered, in a refrigerator. To heat it, place the rice in a microwave-safe bowl, sprinkle with a few drops of water and microwave, loosely covered, for about 2 minutes.

SEV:

These thin, tiny, salted gram flour "noodles" add a lot of crunch to a dish. Let me put it this way: You reach for potato chips, I reach for sev! They have been a part of the street food cuisine of western India for years.

Brands: Haldiram makes an excellent sev—they offer plain salted sev and also many varieties of spiced sev with added nuts, seeds, cornflakes, etc.

How to use it: Sprinkle it on salads, on burgers (page 114), or serve it as is in a bowl alongside a cold beer.

To store: Store in an airtight container.

CHICKPEA FLOUR (BESAN):

A gluten-free flour made from dried ground chickpeas, this flour is a staple in the Indian kitchen. It stands up well to high heat and is often used in a batter for fritters. It is steamed to make fluffy savory cakes, and is also used in desserts. It is added to vegetable dishes and curries to add texture.

JAGGERY:

My only issue with this dried version of boiled sugarcane juice is that I wish stores would sell smaller lumps—even teaching several classes a month, it takes me forever to go through one packet of jaggery! It is used in desserts and drinks, and to sweeten savory lentil dishes. I daresay that it tastes best raw— there is nothing like a nice, sweet lump of jaggery to make you start your day off with a big smile. While you can use brown sugar in a pinch, one taste of sugarcane jaggery and you won't go back. Jaggery is sold in large blocks and it will take you a hammer and a good chisel to break it down into small pieces. Store it in heavy-duty plastic bags.

DAIRY PRODUCTS

PANEER (INDIAN CHEESE):

An extraordinary source of protein, paneer is one of the most versatile Indian ingredients. It is similar in texture and function to very firm tofu. It's a great item to have in your fridge for weeknight meals because it is so easy to prepare. Bricks of paneer, diced paneer, and even deep-fried paneer are now available.

Brands: Nanak brand is the most popular one, sold in 14-ounce packages.

How to use it: It can be fried, grilled, sautéed, or scrambled, in desserts and savory dishes. To grate it, refrigerate it first and then grate on a cheese grater.

To store: Refrigerate and use within five days of opening the package.

YOGURT:

Yogurt, which is milk fermented by specific lactic-acid-producing bacteria, has been used in the Indian kitchen for thousands of years. Homemade yogurt, called *dahi* in India, is traditionally made with rich buffalo milk. It is not just used as a drink or a dessert with fruit—Indians use it as a tenderizer for meats, a souring agent, a base for lightly textured curries, a dessert, and in place of buttermilk. Preparing homemade yogurt is a simple process that does not require any special utensils.

Brands: Indian grocers sell Desi Dahi now, which is very good. If you use Dannon or any other western brand of yogurt, remember two things: Use the plain, not flavored yogurt, and drain the whey before using. If you stir the whey back into the yogurt, it thins it out too much. I have found Greek-style yogurt the perfect consistency for several marinades and desserts, and it does not need to be drained.

How to use it: For marinades, desserts, or drinks you can use whole-milk, low-fat, or fat-free yogurt (drained of whey, of course). For stovetop cooking use whole-milk yogurt and always keep the heat at medium-low, as the yogurt will curdle easily. If it does, there is no way to bring it back!

To store: Refrigerate. The refrigerated shelf life of homemade plain yogurt is about a week. Dishes prepared using yogurt are best eaten fresh; their refrigerated shelf life is a couple of days at most. Freezing of dishes prepared with yogurt is not recommended.

Ghee or clarified butter:

Traditional Indian cooking uses ghee or clarified butter as a cooking medium. Ghee adds richness to the taste of a dish and also provides it a very nutty flavor.

Brands: The best one I have found is Deep.

How to use it: Use it as you would any other cooking oil. It does tend to be heavy, so I would advise using it sparingly, just enough to add flavor. It does solidify as it sits so don't let that worry you. It will become liquid again when it is heated. It is easily available in Indian grocery stores and should be stored in a dark, cool place.

Pomegranate Molasses:

This dark, syrupy product has a tart flavor. Refrigerate any unused portions. It is easily available in most Middle Eastern stores.

RED LENTILS:

These skinless, dried red lentils, called Masoor Dal, are sold in Indian grocery stores. When they are cooked, they turn a pale, creamy yellow. Store them in an airtight container. Rinse them well before you use them.

TAMARIND PASTE:

This is sold in small plastic containers at Indian grocery stores. It is a thick and gooey paste and is extremely tart so do use sparingly. To use it in recipes, dissolve a half teaspoon in a few tablespoons of hot water and then use as needed. Store in a dark, cool place for up to a year.

BEATEN OR FLATTENED RICE:

Beaten rice is called *poha* in India, and looks like white flakes. It is reconstituted using hot water or milk. It should be stored in an airtight container and keeps for up to a year. Available in Indian grocery stores.

PRODUCE

COCONUT FLAKES, PIECES, AND DESICCATED COCONUT:

Indians, particularly in the southern and western parts of India, use a lot of coconut in their cooking. These days many Indian and other Asian grocery stores sell frozen coconut pieces, frozen coconut flakes, and dried coconut flakes. Traditional American grocery stores, I have found, carry only the sweetened flakes that are used in baking. Be sure to check the recipe to see which form you need. Of course, if you are motivated, you can break open a ripe coconut and use a very sharp knife to scrape the fresh white coconut meat from the inside. Be careful though, it is a tricky process, and one slip of the knife and you are in trouble!

Understanding Spices and Herbs
(and other Indian ingredients)

Asafetida (hing): This is a dried resin used very sparingly in cooking. It is added to heated oil and provides a garlicky flavor. It is known for its digestive properties. While raw hing has a pungent odor, earning it the name "stinking spice," or the less-appealing "devil's dung," the smell disappears once it is cooked.

Bay leaves: Bay leaves add a gentle sweetness to dishes. They are not eaten but are cooked with foods to add flavor and removed before serving. Traditional Indian cooking uses *tej patta* (cassia leaf) and many cookbooks suggest using bay leaves as an alternative. I also recommend bay leaves as they are easier to find.

Black or colored peppercorns: These are dried berries of the pepper plant and add a great zing to recipes. You can use them whole, freshly ground, or crushed. You can also use ground white pepper, which is milder than its black counterpart.

Black salt: Honesty first: This is a very funky, pinkish-gray mineral salt that smells like sulfuric acid. That said, it adds a distinctive flavor to dishes and is used in street foods, for topping yogurt, drinks, etc. It is a mineral salt and once it is sprinkled or cooked through, the smell does diffuse. Use very sparingly.

Cardamom pods, green and black: Both types of cardamom are added to sweet and savory dishes. While the green pods are edible raw and whole, the black pods are added to flavor a dish and then removed before serving. You can use your fingers to open a green pod and remove the tiny black seeds inside. Many stores also sell whole and ground cardamom seeds, which are a lot easier to use!

Carom seeds, or bishop's weed: Smaller in size but similar in appearance to cumin seeds, their flavor is similar to a very pungent thyme. They are used to flavor curries, fried dishes (as they are said to aid in digestion), and drinks. You can use them whole or crush them slightly (do not grind them finely) to bring out their flavor. These seeds are called *ajwain* in India.

Cilantro: It has been my experience that people have a love-hate relationship with cilantro. There seems to be no middle ground! Cilantro is one of the most popular herbs in Indian cooking—it is used as a garnish, in chutneys, in curries, and with vegetables. I have never seen it sold dried; unlike dried mint, which is flavorful, dried cilantro has no flavor. Young cilantro stems can be used if they are tender; older stems are thicker and should be discarded. Cilantro lends a lemony flavor to dishes. An important point here: Ground coriander or coriander seeds in any form are *not* a substitute for fresh cilantro.

Cinnamon stick: Used to add a sweet flavor to dishes, it is added to savory and sweet dishes in Indian cooking. It is used in ground as well as whole form. The whole stick is removed after the cooking process as it is not edible. With ground cinnamon, good quality matters and a little goes a long way.

Cloves: Raw cloves are bitter in taste but are used as a mouth freshener in India. Cloves are actually dried flower buds and they add a deep, sweet aroma to dishes.

Coriander seeds: An integral part of Indian cuisine, they are used either whole or ground. Whole seeds are dry-roasted or sizzled in hot oil before use. These seeds impart a distinctive lemony flavor to dishes and provide depth to curries. They are used as a thickening agent in curries. They are often used in unison with cumin seeds.

Cumin seeds: Most Indian dishes that call for *jeera* use the traditional brown cumin seeds (as opposed to the black cumin seed, which is slimmer and is often referred to as *shahi jeera*, or royal cumin). Cumin is used whole or ground. The whole seeds are either dry-roasted or sizzled in hot oil before use. Dry-roasted and ground cumin makes a great garnish for yogurt dishes, rice dishes, and meat curries. It has a strong, smoky, unmistakable taste.

Note: Cumin, sold whole or ground, is a very versatile spice. If you have only whole seeds at home, grind them fresh using a small spice grinder or coffee grinder. You will be able to see and smell the difference between store-bought ground cumin and freshly ground.

Curry leaves: Unfortunately, there is no substitute for these highly aromatic, lemony leaves. They are best used fresh and can be found in Indian and Asian grocery stores. Wrap them in paper towels and refrigerate until needed. You can freeze them to use later but I find the best flavor comes from fresh leaves. They are edible (unlike bay leaves) and are used in curries and chutneys. Some cooks I know like to tear them up before tossing them in curries, claiming the torn leaves add even more flavor.

Fennel seeds: Licorice-flavored, oval fennel seeds are eaten raw, dry-roasted, sizzled in oil, covered in sugar, or ground. Fennel adds great flavor to sweet and savory dishes alike.

Fenugreek leaves, dried: One of the most aromatic and least celebrated of Indian herbs, these leaves are used to flavor vegetables, meats, and rice dishes. A little goes a long way with this herb. Fenugreek seeds are definitely not a substitute for the dried leaves.

Fenugreek seeds: Small, flat, and yellowish brown in appearance, these seeds are used to add a savory flavor to curries and pickles. Use these bitter-tasting seeds with a miser's touch. While the bitterness does dissipate as the seeds are cooked, don't add more than a touch.

Garam Masala: This is a very popular spice mix in India and involves grinding together cloves, cumin seeds, green cardamom pods, black cardamom pods, cinnamon, coriander seeds, black peppercorns, bay leaves, and nutmeg. Each household generally has its own special proportions, much as Italians have their own versions of pasta sauce. Stores generally sell ground garam masala. I once participated in a test by the *Washington Post* on different varieties of garam masala in the market. Sprinkle over prepared dishes like lentils or curries just before serving, as a flavor builder. It adds a heady aroma and a deep earthy flavor. Use sparingly as a little goes a long way.

Mango powder, dried (*amchur*): Sun-dried green mangoes are ground to create this tangy ground spice that lends a (what else?) tangy taste to curries! You can substitute lemon juice for mango powder. It does have a distinctive sour flavor, though, so do give it a try if you can. Fresh mango puree is not a substitute.

Mustard seeds, black: Sizzled in hot oil or ground in a wet paste, mustard seeds add a very pungent, distinctive flavor to dishes. These seeds are small and round in appearance. Do not substitute American mustard here.

Onion seeds or nigella: These are called *kalonji* in India and it is under that name that you will find them at the Indian store. Although they are referred to as onion seeds, they have no relationship to any onion plant! This spice adds a smoky and peppery flavor to a dish. They are rarely eaten raw; they must be either dry-roasted or sizzled in oil to help the seeds release their flavor. Use sparingly, as too much can make a dish bitter.

Pomegranate seeds, dried: These add a lovely crunch and a tangy flavor to dishes. Depending on the recipe you may be able to use fresh seeds, but please consult the recipe carefully for this. The converse is not true—dried seeds cannot be used in place of fresh pomegranate seeds. Many Indian stores also sell a dried pomegranate seed powder called *anardana* powder. It can be sprinkled on dishes to lend a tangy flavor.

Red chiles, whole dried and powdered, or red chile flakes: These add heat, flavor, and pizzazz to food. Use according to your tastes. I never fail to advise my students to start with a little; you can always add more but you cannot take it out once it is added. I love using red chile flakes in my dishes instead of the powder as the flakes not only add taste but make for a lovely presentation. You can use cayenne if you cannot find red chile powder. Please note that Indian red chile powder is *not* the same as American chili powder, which is an amalgamation of various spices and herbs.

Dried red chiles: Many recipes in this book call for dried red chiles. They are deep red in color and about 4 inches in length. I recommend the Deep brand. You can buy these at the Indian grocery stores or at www.grocerybabu.com. Basically, dried red chiles are green cayenne chiles that have been dried in the sun.

To use these, break them into two or three pieces. While there are several varieties of chiles available, I recommend and use this one as it is the easiest to find. If you cannot find the whole dried red chiles, you can use crushed red pepper flakes. An alternative is *chile de arbol*.

Saffron: Saffron, the world's most expensive spice, is actually an affordable luxury since a little goes a long way. Saffron filaments are the dried stigmas of the saffron flower and it takes 225,000 stigmas, picked from 75,000 violet crocuses during the two-week fall flowering period, to produce one pound of saffron. As a general rule, I use about three strands per person in a recipe. Saffron is water soluble and the best way to use it is to soak it in warm water or milk for a few minutes to allow the spice to release its color and fragrance. Please note that turmeric is *not* a substitute and neither is orange-red food coloring, which may provide the color but not the fragrance of saffron.

Sesame seeds: Toast these tiny cream-colored seeds to add an earthy, nutty flavor to dishes.

Star anise: Used whole, this adds a lovely and very strong licorice flavor to dishes. It is not eaten whole, and is removed after the cooking process. I often use this lovely star-shaped spice to garnish curries, rice dishes, and desserts.

Turmeric: Turmeric is what gives Indian food its distinctive yellow color. It has been known for its antiseptic and anti-inflammatory properties. It is to be used sparingly; too much will make a dish bitter. Turmeric is a rhizome and fresh turmeric is also used in Indian cooking. The powder and the fresh root are not substitutes for each other. Only the powder is used in this book.

MONICA'S SPICE AND HERB USAGE GUIDELINES FOR *MODERN SPICE*

Indian cuisine cannot be standardized; there is as much creativity in Indian food as there are cooks out there! However, there are many people who are just getting introduced to spices and want guidelines on how much of a spice they should be using in a recipe. I have this discussion with my students all the time. If I say you should use a pinch of saffron, a dash of black salt, or a teaspoon of cumin, they ask, "Where does it say that? How do you know?"

I have created a simple guide, "A Spice and Herb Bowl," for novices and occasional cooks, who might be trying their hand at Indian food for the first time and are intimidated by the complexity of the spices involved. Once you become familiar with the proportion of spices in relation to dishes and what they can do for you, you won't need this guide at all.

This bowl gives amounts for a dish for four; you can increase the amounts proportionally for more servings. However, the bowl does not show the succession in which spices are added; that is dependent on the specific recipe that you are using. **This bowl shows proportions:** For instance, for a dish made with one head of cauliflower, you would use a pinch of hing, a few pieces of whole spices, and ⅛ to ½ teaspoon of salt and red chile. I don't know of too many recipes intended for four to six that use tablespoons of turmeric; generally less than a teaspoon size is appropriate. Clearly, the spice bowl is meant for basic recipes: If you are preparing a dish of, say, mustard fish for four, you may use a lot of mustard, but you probably will still only use a touch of turmeric and other spices. Or if you are making cinnamon rice, you may add more cinnamon but will not, I hope, add tablespoons of saffron or loads of cumin.

Now some thoughts before you dig into the bowl:

1. Follow the recipe exactly the first time. All these recipes are well tested and will give you an idea of what the dish is supposed to taste like.

2. Play with the recipe the second time you make it. If you like curry leaves, add more; if you hate them, leave them out. Same goes with cilantro or cumin.

There is no way for me to know how much heat you can take in a dish, so I have recommended medium heat levels; add more or less if you like.

3. You will learn how ingredients like asafetida or turmeric or mustard seeds affect a dish. Once you are comfortable with their roles, play with them. Mustard seeds, for instance, can be sizzled in oil or soaked in water and then ground to a paste to be used in curries. The possibilities are endless.

THE SPICE AND HERB BOWL FOR *MODERN SPICE*

A few pieces –
Cinnamon, Bay Leaves,
Cloves, Cardamom,
Peppercorns, Star Anise

Less than a teaspoon –
Red Chile, Salt, Black Salt,
Chaat Masala, Garam Masala,
Dried Mango Powder, Ginger
Powder, Turmeric

A pinch – Hing, Mace,
Nutmeg, Saffron,
Fenugreek Seeds

Tablespoons – Ground Coriander
Tandoori Masala,
Fresh Ginger,
Fresh Garlic,
Dried Fenugreek Leaves,
Ground Cumin, Curry
Powder, Spice Mixes

A teaspoon – Mustard Seeds, Cumin Seeds,
Onion Seeds, Bishops Weed (Ajwain),
Fennel, Dried Pomegranate Seeds, Jaggery

As you wish – Fresh Herbs: Cilantro, Mint, Basil,
Curry Leaves, etc.; Coconut Milk, Grated Coconut,
Green Chile, Onion, extra Red Chile. (Cayenne is
added to taste as well.)

MONICA'S KITCHEN RULES

I always share these rules with students of my cooking classes and want to share them with you as well.

1. Use fresh spices. Don't use spices that have been sitting in your cupboard since last Thanksgiving.

2. Use nonstick cookware where possible; in Indian food we don't deglaze pans to prepare sauces. Nonstick uses less oil and I find the food cooks faster.

3. For all the recipes here, I have used a regular gas stove, and the recipes have been tested on the largest burner (by me and by all the testers).

4. Don't substitute without checking. Coriander seeds are not a substitute for fresh coriander leaves (that is, cilantro); curry powder is not a substitute for curry leaves. I have provided tips and hints throughout the book to help you.

5. Watch the salt. In my cooking classes, I routinely leave out salt from at least a couple of dishes. Ninety-nine percent of the students don't notice even after tasting the food. Fresh spices add a lot of flavor, and I find myself using less and less salt.

6. Don't *under*cook meats and poultry. Indian cooking really does not make use of rare or medium cooked meats; meat is always cooked thoroughly.

7. Do not *over*cook vegetables. If you do, they will be soggy and limp and worse, they will have lost their taste and nutritional value. Use fresh vegetables whenever possible.

8. The recipes in this book all have moderate spice levels and, unless otherwise indicated, moderate heat levels. You can always add, but you cannot subtract!

9. Cooking, at least to me, is all about understanding what ingredients can do for you. You will notice that most recipes in this book use very few spices. A few flavorful spices used in the right proportion do all the work so you don't have to. You really don't need long and complicated ingredient lists to make a tasty

dinner. I have always said that simplicity has a lot of charm, and with spices, a lot of flavor.

10. Read the whole recipe before cooking. It will give you a better sense of what to expect and how to manage your time and ingredients.

11. Don't leave out the garnishes. They not only make the dish look attractive and add oomph but many times they add the final fillip of flavor, that little touch that makes all the difference.

12. When cooking with nuts, taste them before adding to the dish. I find that nuts often go rancid since people tend to store them for a long time.

13. Have your spices and other ingredients lined up and ready to go before you cook. When the oil is shimmering hot, it is a bad time to go hunt down your box of cumin seeds!

So now that you know the rules of the house, let's get cooking!

CHUTNEYS and MARINADES

. . . .

Next to grandmothers (and mothers, of course), street vendors in India make the best chutneys. There is something so enticing about the way they add chutneys and dried spices on top of pan-fried potato cakes or over yogurt-bathed lentil dumplings.

Once, I gathered up the nerve to ask an old vendor in Delhi who makes the most amazing *tikkis* (potato cakes filled with onions, cilantro, and baby peas, then topped with a tangy green chile chutney and a dab of cilantro chutney) how he made his chutney. He looked at me thoughtfully for a moment and then said, "*Madam: Ghoda ghass se yaari karega to khayega kya?*" Translation: Madam, if a horse becomes friends with the grass [hay], what will he eat to live? Point taken: His chutneys are a trade secret. But not one to give up easily, I pressed on. Finally he said, "*Aachi chijze dalo aur dil khol ke dalo,*" wise words. Use good ingredients and use them with an open heart, very liberally!

In my grandmother's house in Multan (part of India before the separation and now a city in Pakistan) before I was born, the most popular chutney, my father tells me, was mint chutney made in what was called a "*davri-sota.*" A sota is a wooden stick two to three inches in diameter and about two feet tall. A davri is a piece of hollowed solid granite, eight to twelve inches in diameter. Grandma would first add onions to the granite davri and use the sota to mash them. Then she added green chiles, mint leaves, green mango, and spices like carom seeds, red chiles, and dried pomegranate seeds. A bit of salt and sugar would be the final touch. Dad constantly regales us with stories of when one of his uncles, visiting from America in the 1970s, brought home something called a "Molly baby," a steel hand grinder. They tried to make chutneys in it, but no one approved of the taste; to them the granite-ground chutneys had an earthy flavor that was lost in the steel blades of the grinder.

We have come a long way today from davri-sota and Molly baby! I love to make my chutneys in a small blender, which is one of the most used appliances in my house—and I love their taste.

Chutneys, once used in India just for toppings to add extra flavors, have found a new home in Indian kitchens today. I use them as marinades, in making curries, for spreads on sandwiches, and even as a topping for cheese.

This chapter provides simple recipes that will surely become staples in your kitchen, and also introduces a unique way of using chutneys as marinades and sauces (and elsewhere in the book they'll be cross-referenced for use in curries and even in desserts).

With these recipes, I'm sharing some of my all-time favorites. Use these as a foundation to create your own favorites, ones that satisfy your unique taste buds! As the old vendor said: Use your ingredients with an open heart. Play with them, add some, remove some, and you will come up with a mixture that will become your own trade secret.

CHUTNEY BASICS

There really are no rules when it comes to making chutneys; it really is all up to your taste buds! But there are a few simple guidelines that will help you create the best possible flavors, regardless of the combination of ingredients used.

1. The number one rule is to use the freshest ingredients possible, especially when you are creating raw chutneys. For cooked recipes, frozen vegetables and canned fruits are acceptable. In all honesty, there is one chutney I buy all the time instead of making it at home—and that is tamarind-date chutney, because the tamarind used in making chutneys is already a preserved ingredient (that is, we are not using fresh tamarind).

2. Make sure you have all the ingredients ready before you begin, especially for cooked chutneys. Spices tend to burn easily, so you won't have time once the cooking has started to look around for other ingredients.

3. Always use fresh herbs and spices. Use your nose to judge freshness: If you cannot smell the herb or spice, discard it. Herbs and spices that have lost their potency will not only affect the taste of the chutney, but may also cause tummy ailments. I generally never buy a mint or a cilantro chutney because it is the freshness of the herbs that make the chutney taste good.

4. Always cook and store chutneys in nonreactive pans and bowls, preferably stainless steel or glass. Other types of metal react with the acid in chutneys, giving them a metallic taste.

5. Be sure to use a clean dry spoon to dip into your prepared chutney. Moisture can cause mold to form in the chutneys.

6. Make small portions of raw chutneys, since they have a limited shelf life.

7. Experiment. Use the recipes provided as a template to create your own spectrum of flavors. There really is no right or wrong combination.

MINT-CILANTRO CHUTNEY

MAKES *1 cup*

PREP TIME: *5 minutes*

1 cup packed cilantro
(leaves and stems; see
Note)

1 cup packed mint (leaves
only, please)

1 green serrano chile
(optional; if you don't
like too much heat,
remove the seeds)

¼ small red onion, peeled
and sliced

1 tablespoon dried
pomegranate seeds
(optional)

2 tablespoons fresh lemon
juice

½ teaspoon table salt

Up to 2 tablespoons water

This is the most popular chutney in India, hands down. It can be found in many Indian-American homes, in restaurants, and now in jars on grocery store shelves. Its charm lies in how simple it is to prepare. My father always adds a little yogurt to his chutney to make it creamy and then pairs it with lamb kebabs. My mom-in-law adds a hearty dose of roasted peanuts and serves it with savory snacks; Mom adds pomegranate seeds—you get the idea—to each his own.

This versatile chutney has so many uses. Thin it a little and use it as a salad dressing for a crisp green salad; use it in the consistency provided here as a spread on a baguette topped with fresh cucumber slices; or simply drizzle it on some freshly grilled fish for a fresh flavor.

One word of advice here: Green chutneys have a short shelf life. Make them in small batches and make them often—they only take a few minutes but the rewards are well worth the effort (which really isn't much).

. . . .

1. Blend the cilantro, mint, chile, onion, pomegranate seeds (if using), lemon juice, and salt in a blender to a smooth paste. To aid in the blending process, you can add up to 2 tablespoons of water, if needed. Taste and add more salt if needed.

2. Transfer to a covered container and chill for about 30 minutes.

3. Serve cool. This chutney will keep, refrigerated, for 4 days.

Note: If you are using fresh, young cilantro sprigs the stems are tender and are fine to use in the chutney. If the sprigs are older, the stems tend to be tough and should be discarded.

Did you know . . . cilantro is not a substitute for coriander. Coriander seeds are used in whole or ground form to add texture and lemony flavor to a dish. Cilantro, the fresh herb that grows from coriander seeds, adds a completely different texture and flavor. Our old gardener used to say that coriander seeds are shameless—you have to crush them with your shoe before you plant them or they won't bloom!

RED PEPPER AND GREEN TOMATILLO CHUTNEY

MAKES *1 generous cup*

PREP/COOK TIME: *40 minutes*

2 tablespoons vegetable oil

5 or 6 fresh curry leaves

Pinch of asafetida

½ teaspoon cumin seeds

½ teaspoon fenugreek seeds

1 teaspoon fennel seeds

1 teaspoon onion seeds

½ teaspoon black mustard seeds

4 whole dried red chiles

2 cups diced green tomatillos (10 to 12 medium tomatillos)

1 cup seeded and diced red bell pepper (1 medium pepper)

2 teaspoons grated peeled fresh ginger

¼ cup sugar

½ cup water

¼ cup white vinegar or fresh lemon juice

½ teaspoon table salt

I used to love a spiced green tomato entrée with unusual elements like onion seeds and fenugreek that a friend would make for me. I tarted up the recipe a bit and converted it into a yummy and tangy chutney.

This chutney has a bit more liquid than most chutneys. I like it this way to spoon it over entrées. If you like a thicker consistency, allow the chutney to simmer a bit longer.

. . . .

1. In a medium skillet, heat the vegetable oil. When the oil begins to shimmer, add the curry leaves, asafetida, and the cumin, fenugreek, fennel, onion, and mustard seeds. As soon as the seeds begin to sizzle, about 1 minute, add the chiles, tomatillos, bell pepper, ginger, and sugar. Mix well.

2. Add the water and vinegar and bring to a boil. Reduce the heat to medium-low and continue on a gentle simmer for about 35 minutes, until the tomatillos and the bell pepper are soft and the liquid is syrupy.

3. Add the salt. Mix well.

4. Remove from the heat. Remove the whole chiles, if you like. Transfer to a container and cool.

5. Cover and refrigerate until needed.

Note: Be careful when using fenugreek seeds. They add bitterness to a dish, so a little goes a long way. Also, they are not substitutes for fresh fenugreek or dried fenugreek leaves; the flavors and textures are miles apart.

MANGO-ALMOND CHUTNEY

This chutney is good over plain crackers for a divine and delicious appetizer. Take care to use mangoes that are ripe but not overripe and mushy. They should be firm to the touch. I prefer not to use canned mangoes for this recipe, as the chutney loses texture. If you cannot find fresh mangoes and decide that you must use canned mangoes, drain them first, leave out the sugar from the recipe, and cut down on the cooking time, as they are already pretty soft.

. . . .

1. In a bowl, combine the mangoes, raisins, ginger, and sugar. Set aside.

2. In a deep saucepan, heat the vegetable oil. When the oil begins to shimmer, add the fennel and cumin seeds, the curry powder, and chiles. Sauté for about 1 minute or until the spices begin to sizzle.

3. Add the mango mixture and almonds and continue to cook for 2 to 3 minutes or until the sugar begins to melt. Add the vinegar, fruit juice, and salt. Bring to a gentle boil and simmer on medium heat for 20 to 30 minutes or until the mixture has thickened.

4. Cool, then transfer to a covered container. Refrigerate until needed.

Did you know . . . several cultures consider almonds a fertility charm?

MAKES *2 cups*
PREP/COOK TIME: *40 minutes*

2½ cups ¼-inch diced peeled mangoes (2 to 3 mangoes)
½ cup golden raisins
1 teaspoon grated peeled fresh ginger
¼ cup sugar
1 tablespoon vegetable oil
½ teaspoon fennel seeds
½ teaspoon cumin seeds
½ teaspoon store-bought hot Madras curry powder
2 dried red chiles, broken into pieces
¼ cup slivered blanched almonds
⅓ cup white vinegar
½ cup fresh orange juice or pineapple juice
½ teaspoon table salt

FENNEL-CHILE DRY RUB

MAKES *about ¼ cup*

PREP/COOK TIME: *5 minutes*

¼ cup fennel seeds

4 whole dried red chiles

½ teaspoon ground
   peppercorns (use a
   medley of different
   colored peppercorns)

This is a wonderful rub for meats and fish. While I prefer it as a dry rub, you can add lemon juice or a neutral oil like grapeseed to make it wet if you like. Use the rub on your choice of meat, allow it to marinate for a few minutes, and then grill, roast, or sauté. As with any spice, if you are going to store this for a long time, please ensure it is still flavorful before using. Use your nose—if you can smell the spices, it is still good to go; if not, toss it and make a fresh batch. This rub lasts up to two months in a sealed container.

. . . .

1. Heat a small dry skillet over medium heat. Add the fennel seeds. Toss until the seeds are fragrant. This takes just about 1 minute, so watch them carefully and keep tossing the seeds in the pan or they will burn.

2. Add the chiles and toss for another 5 seconds.

3. Remove from heat and allow to cool.

4. Grind to a coarse powder in a spice grinder. Add the peppercorns and mix well.

5. Store, covered, until needed.

Did you know . . . chewing raw fennel seeds is a great digestive, and is said to be an aphrodisiac! Fennel is often confused with anise. It has a licorice-like flavor and is used raw or toasted.

KUMQUAT AND MANGO CHUTNEY WITH ONION SEEDS

MAKES *1½ cups*
PREP/COOK TIME: *45 minutes*

We love kumquats in our house but my son, who calls them *chota santra* (little orange) often complains about their tartness. I wondered how they would lend themselves to a chutney. The answer came to me in this chutney, where I use the tremendous sweetness of Alphonso mango puree to balance the kumquats' tartness. This is great to top grilled chicken, pork, and even grilled fish.

. . . .

2 tablespoons vegetable oil
1 teaspoon onion seeds
1 teaspoon fennel seeds
1 dry pint kumquats, pitted and sliced (with skin)
¾ teaspoon red chile powder or red chile flakes
1 cup sugar
1 cup Alphonso mango puree (see Note)
½ cup white vinegar
Table salt

1. Heat the oil in a deep saucepan. When the oil begins to shimmer, add the onion and fennel seeds. As soon as they begin to sizzle, add the kumquats, chile powder, sugar, mango puree, and vinegar and stir well to combine.

2. Cook on medium heat, stirring occasionally, for 30 minutes or until the mixture has thickened and the kumquats are soft. Add salt to taste.

3. Refrigerate in an airtight jar for up to 3 weeks.

Note: For Alphonso mango puree I drain 6 to 8 slices of mango from a can of Ratna brand Alphonso mango slices and place them in a bowl. I crush them with my hands—it takes very little effort, as they are already very soft. This should give you about a cup, depending on the size of the slices. Adjust quantity as needed to come up with 1 cup.

Did you know . . . the George W. Bush administration is credited with legalizing the import of Alphonso mangoes to the United States.

Ginger and Honey Marinade

MAKES *3 generous tablespoons*

PREP/COOK TIME: *5 minutes*

1 tablespoon grated peeled fresh ginger

¼ cup warmed liquid honey

1 teaspoon red chile flakes

1 tablespoon pomegranate molasses

1 tablespoon vegetable oil

½ teaspoon grated lime or lemon zest

You will fall in love with this easy marinade. It is just perfect for chicken wings. For this recipe, try to use fresh ginger, which is easily available. Jarred ginger, which I am a great supporter of for curries, just will not do this marinade justice. I don't add any salt to this marinade, as I use it in so many different ways. For instance, I use it as a sauce over already salted Pan-Seared Eggplant (page 130).

. . . .

Combine all the ingredients in a bowl and stir thoroughly to combine. Transfer to a covered, nonreactive container and refrigerate until needed.

Note: Pomegranate molasses is easily available at Middle Eastern grocery stores, Indian stores, and online. If you cannot find it, you can make your own by reducing pomegranate juice mixed with equal amounts of sugar and lemon juice. Simmer until the mixture has a syrupy consistency. If you cannot find it and don't make your own, leave it out of the recipe and add a tablespoon of lemon juice instead.

POMEGRANATE CHUTNEY

"It had to happen," my husband said when I first served him this. My love of everything pomegranate is legendary in our household. I love everything about it—the color, the taste, the texture. Everything except coaxing out the seeds—and that is why I have, politely, shown my hubby how to do it! This chutney has more of a sauce consistency. I just drizzle it over grilled pork chops or chicken and have also used it in place of lemon juice when I make a fruit salad. Use this chutney within two days.

. . . .

Place the pomegranate seeds, lemon juice, ginger, chaat masala, and brown sugar in a food processor and grind to a coarse paste or puree. (You can pass the paste through a sieve for a finer texture and use the sauce as a salad dressing.) Add salt to taste. Transfer to a covered container and refrigerate until needed.

MAKES ½ cup
PREP/COOK TIME: 5 minutes (15 if you need to coax the seeds out of the pomegranate!)

1 cup fresh pomegranate seeds
1 tablespoon fresh lemon juice
¼ teaspoon minced peeled fresh ginger
½ teaspoon store-bought chaat masala
1 tablespoon light brown sugar
Table salt

PINEAPPLE-LENTIL RELISH

MAKES *2¼ cups (serving size is about 2 to 3 tablespoons per person)*

PREP/COOK TIME: *About 1 hour*

1 cup dried red lentils

3 ¼ cups water

¼ cup superfine sugar

3 tablespoons plus 2 drops
    fresh lemon juice

2 cups canned crushed
    pineapple with juice

1 teaspoon minced peeled
    fresh ginger

1 teaspoon ground cumin

Table salt

Red chile powder or red
    chile flakes

Chef Stefan Jarausch, executive chef at The Madison, in Washington, D.C., gave me this mild-tasting, unusual combination of fruit and lentils a couple of years ago when I was bored with the same old, same old relishes around Thanksgiving. Yes, we celebrate Thanksgiving. While it is not a traditionally Indian holiday, our kids, nieces, nephews, and young friends who are born and raised in the United States celebrate it as their own.

. . . .

1. In a deep saucepan, bring the lentils and 3 cups of the water to a rolling boil over high heat. Scum will form on the surface. Skim it off with a spoon and discard. Boil the lentils for 3 to 4 minutes. Reduce the heat to medium-low and cook for 5 to 7 minutes or until the lentils are soft. Drain and set aside.

2. While the lentils are cooking, prepare the pineapple mixture: In an 8- to 10-inch nonreactive skillet, combine the sugar, ¼ cup water, and 2 drops of lemon juice. Bring to a boil. Cook for 10 to 12 minutes, stirring frequently, until the syrup turns a light brown. This will happen suddenly, so keep watch, as it can burn easily.

3. Add the pineapple, 3 tablespoons lemon juice, ginger, and cumin. Reduce the heat and simmer slowly until all remaining liquid is reduced to a syrupy consistency and has almost all evaporated. This should take about 25 minutes.

4. Remove from the heat. Add the lentils to the pineapple mixture. Warm through and season with salt and chile powder as desired. Serve warm. Can be refrigerated for a week.

Food, Father, and Faith

· ·

I wish I had the gift to recall my very early years with more clarity. My earliest memory of my father is foggy. I am standing on what appears to be a cobbled path, my tiny feet just steps away from a stream of flowing water. He is walking toward me with something in his hands. I have been waiting for a long time. My mother tells me I used to wait for him at that very spot every day when I was four. I cannot remember every day, but I do remember that one day. I remember a very tall, very slim man with a big mustache and an even bigger smile holding out his large hand in front of me. As he opens his hand, I see the treat I have been waiting for——an offering, my mother told me, from a local Jaipur temple. Tiny little balls of bliss——sugar-soaked deep-fried orange pearls made of chickpea flour. I take as many as my tiny hands can hold and stuff the orange pearls into my mouth.

And then, my first memory of my father fades.

I am seven in my strongest childhood memory. I think I had decided to figure out how his brand-new Sony stereo system worked. I can see myself sitting in the middle of the living room with a completely disassembled system around me, terrified. He was angry when he saw the mess, really angry. When he calmed down, he showed me how to fix the system. The stereo never quite sounded the same. Of course, the time he remembers the best might be when, as a science experiment, I set fire to my mother's kitchen curtains to test how long it took nylon to burn. Or maybe when I placed all the wristwatches in the house under running water to see which ones were waterproof. Most of the time he helped me fix what I broke.

My father is not an overly religious man, but he did (and still continues to) pray with some regularity and would often pile the whole family into the car on Friday mornings (Fridays are the weekend where I grew up in the Middle East) and take us to the local Hindu temple or the Sikh *gurudwara*. I cannot say that I totally enjoyed the experience when I was very young; I did not understand a word of what was being said by the priests. They spoke in either Sanskrit or pure Punjabi (at the Sikh temple) and I was always lost. I went because, I guess, I was greedy—I loved the *prasad*, the sweets that were offered to gods and then distributed to the devotees. The Sikh temple in particular offered what is called a *langar*, a free meal for anyone who came in, and I would wait and wait for it each Friday. Luscious lentils, pickles with cucumbers, potatoes with varying spices and handmade breads—what could be better?

When we visited India over the summers, specifically Delhi where my family lived, each Tuesday my grandfather would head to the Hanuman Temple. All of us cousins would wait for him to come back home with treats from the temple. He would bring back not only offerings but extra boxes of sweets that all the kids could share and enjoy. "I love the prasad from the temples," I would declare loudly, clapping my hands with typical childish enthusiasm. He offered to take me around to some of the temples. Busy with cousins and play, I refused but added, "Just bring us back the prasad." I

don't remember saying that. Honestly, I don't. My mother reminded me of those words when we were talking about religion and my struggle to make my own son understand about temples and the Hindu religion.

As I grew older, my attitude toward temples bothered my father. "Going to the temples is not just about the food and the prasad, Monica. You need to learn how to pray and be respectful to the religion." But I was sixteen and having nothing of this talk. I rebelled and was, in hindsight, perhaps a little cruel. "I don't understand your temples, Dad. Why don't they speak a language we can all understand? What is the point in going there when I cannot understand anything? I don't mind praying, but who should I pray to? There are so many gods; which is mine? What is it with Hindu religion and women anyway? Why are women treated as second-class citizens in the *Ramayan* and the *Mahabharat?*" This is one memory that I do have that is very clear. I had never spoken to my father in that tone before. I was angry and upset. How could a decent man with such good morals and great spirituality ask his kids to follow a religion they did not understand? Then I remember saying, "Perhaps I should convert to Baha'i, Dad. At least I understand their simple rules." I don't remember his reaction. My mother told me, years later, that he had been inconsolable.

A few weeks passed with no mention of temples or gurudwaras, and Dad told us that we were going to Kashmir to enjoy some of the wonderful cuisine the area had to offer and to travel around the northern parts of India. We were a family obsessed with food, and this sounded like a great plan to all of us—my mother, my younger sister, and even my grandpa, my Dad's father, who decided to join us on the trip.

We started our journey in Srinagar by staying in a gorgeous *shikara* boat on the Dal Lake. The old man who was cooking on the boat made us one delight after another—lamb cooked in aromatic curries, rice cooked with lamb and nuts, innumerable sides. I was in food heaven. I don't think we ate at restaurants but a handful of times that entire visit because the food on the boat was so amazing.

Then Dad announced we were going to Katra and on to Vaishno Devi Maa's temple. I was stunned. When did this happen? But Dad had his way—thankfully, I say in hindsight. I agreed to go, thinking well, the food will be great even if I don't understand or agree with what will be going on.

I remember getting to the base of the mountain where the temple is located. It is a several mile trek up the mountain to get to the cave where Vaishno Devi Maa, a very important Goddess in the Hindu religion, had her home. As we began the walk, the atmosphere around us seemed to change radically. Leaving a noisy town we were suddenly on a path filled with devotees of every shape and size imaginable. People with crutches, with small babies, and really old grandmothers—many of them intentionally barefoot—were walking up the rough road to have a *darshan*, to be able to pray to the Mother in the Holy Cave. As we were walking up, several people were remarking that one does not just show up here, Mother Vaishno Devi always sends an invitation—"You are here because you are invited." The devotees were singing and praying and shouting "*Jai*

Mata Di," praise be to the Mother. I had never seen anything like it in my life. They were wearing small red or pink scarves with ornate gold lace, and one of them offered me a scarf. I was thrilled and pretty soon found myself joining the devotees and shouting along with them.

We reached the top of the small mountain and were able to go down a tiny tunnel into the Holy Cave and offer prayers. Dad and Mom were in tears and so was I. I don't remember why I cried. I really don't. I just remember that it felt so good.

I remember a very giddy feeling of belonging; of finally understanding my father and his beliefs, even with all my overly analytical and logical questions. Recently, on a trip to India, I talked to my Dad about our visit to Vaishno Devi Maa and he said, "You needed to learn what faith is and that trip showed it to you."

Oh, I know we must have been offered food in the form of *prasad* at the end of our visit to the Vaishno Devi Maa temple, as is customary in all temples. I don't remember it. ☀

MODERN DRINKS

While most people assume Indians to be teetotalers, alcohol has always been part of the culture; references to *madira* (wine) can be found in many Indian texts that are hundreds of years old. *Sura* (alcohol) has been found in documentation as old as 4 B.C.; incidentally Sura was also the name of the Indian goddess of alcohol or wine. Some temples in Rajasthan such as the Shila Devi Mandir in Jaipur give a *prasad* (blessing of the gods to the devotee) of local liquor (see www.mandirnet.org) and although not intoxicating, liquid homeopathic medications have an alcohol base.

Urdu poetry gave wine the title of *Angur ki Beti* (daughter of the grape) while modern Indian poets like the late Harivansh Rai Bachan have written scintillating and spectacular poetry on the topic of drinking and wine houses.

In India today still some of the old forms of liquor are popular among the rural people like *taddi* (palm liquor) and *feni* (a cashew nut liquor). I would venture to say that the most common form of liquor consumed in rural India was, and I am sure still is, *tharra*, or country liquor, which is produced by fermenting sugarcane juice. It is a very potent and unrefined form of alcohol; think moonshine.

My father tells this story about his earliest experience with local Indian alcohol in the 1960s:

I had some American customers visiting my company in Jaipur who expressed a desire to see some of the historic places around. We took them to Rajwara, which was about 100 kilometers from Jaipur. The local rajaa (king) was well known to the owners of our company and he hosted a dinner for our group. We all assembled in the diwan (main room) for a drink before proceeding to the dining hall. The rajaa asked us if we'd like some real Indian liquor. The consensus was, of course, yes, and the Americans were eager, too. We sat around a round table and tall transparent glasses were placed in front of each of us. Then the rajaa asked his servants to fill up these glasses with water almost to the brim. He asked his butler to get the pitcher of liquor and some quarter-inch round glass rods. The liquor was in an earthen pot whose mouth was covered with cloth. The rajaa took a glass stick and dipped it into the pitcher; what came out was some sort of a thick syrup. He proceeded to place these sticks in our individual glasses and asked us to stir gently. Then, standing up, he proposed a toast but advised us to sip slowly. Our foreign guests thought it was some sort of a joke and they drank the whole glass in one go. Most of them had to be carried home! Such was the potency of homemade Indian liquor.

Some diluted forms of this kind of liquor are produced in Rajasthan in distilleries even today. The popular ones are known as Royal Kesar Kasturi and Royal Jagmohan.

Over the past hundred years or so, at least partly thanks to the British influence, Indians have gravitated toward Scotch and whiskey. *Peena Pilaana* (drinking and serving drinks) is one of the oldest forms of entertainment (although I cannot provide a carbon dating to the origin of intoxication). The Indian habit of being overly polite and not wanting to inconvenience their host by saying "*Kuch Nahin*" (nothing) when asked, "What will you have to drink?" resulted in a smart marketer coming out with a brand of Scotch whisky called, you guessed it, Kuch Nahin.

Indians are famous for their *sharbats* (sweetened nonalcoholic drinks) featuring fruits like *santara* (orange), and *annanas* (pineapple), and their extraordinary touch with juices of pomegranate, mango, and more. But sadly, for years the only beverage on Indian restaurant menus in the United States was either hot tea or some type of lassi. Now, I don't know about you, but I've seen enough recipes of mango lassi to last me a lifetime and then some! Thankfully, there has been a change in the recent past; this change in the Indian cocktail culture is making itself known on various restaurant menus—Washington, D.C.'s, Indique Heights shows off its jaggery-based martini and Bombay Club offers a mango Bellini; Chicago's Vermillion offers an amazing wine list. And in Indian American households, people are whipping up all kinds of concoctions. There is even a flourishing Indian vineyard, Sula Vineyards in Nasik, started by a young professional who used to work in the Silicon Valley; wine tastings held at Indian restaurants like Tabla in New York include Sula wines.

Mangoes are not for lassis anymore; think martinis. Tamarind is not for souring curries anymore; think margaritas. This chapter includes great cocktails with a truly modern Indian taste.

Meeting My Indian Idol

Sanjeev Kapoor is a name that evokes sighs and ooohs and aahhhs in our circle. If you don't know who he is, you are missing out! Sanjeev is an Indian chef who rose to fame in the 1990s; he made it fashionable to cook and be seen cooking. Sanjeev has the longest running television show in the history of Indian television. I often refer to him as India's Emeril Lagasse, but really he is India's Emeril and Rachael Ray rolled into one. Until Sanjeev Kapoor came on the scene, cooking was considered a menial task. If a kid told his parents he was going to go to culinary school, the response was generally not polite. *"Bawarchi banega kya?"* (You will be a cook?)—implying really that you would be a cook in someone's home, a servant.

I remember as a child I would love to go into the kitchen and watch the servants cooking, sometimes with my grandma but mostly without her; it bothered everyone in the house a great deal. "Why is she always in there with the servants? Tell her to come out." Today, I laugh when non-Indian people say to me, "Teach me to cook the way that they do in India." Well, many Indians in the middle and upper classes do not cook alone—their servants act as sous chefs! In our house, I always remember having a cook. Always. When my first book was released, my cousin called me to tell me that she had tried two recipes and loved them. "But you don't cook," I said to her. "Oh, I marked the ones I wanted and read them to the cook. He made them."

Yes, cooking as a profession was not looked upon with much respect.

Sanjeev broke the stereotype. It's not that there weren't or aren't other great chefs in India, but most of them are not "everyman's" chef. Sanjeev, with his soft words, easy demeanor, and charming smile, made it fun and honorable to be in the kitchen. His shows began to develop a cult following. Housewives (and, secretly, their husbands), new brides, moms-in-law, and armchair cooks all began to tune into the show. It was followed by cookbooks, radio spots, more TV shows, and now even a food channel. His spices and chutney mixes began to take hold on shelves that had forever sold the same classic MTR and MDH brands. (Think Emeril's spices versus McCormick or a Trader Joe's brand.) I loved watching him—he had *fun* in the kitchen. He laughed and smiled and made cooking look like what it should be: a pleasurable, approachable experience.

Several years ago, I interviewed him for an article for the *New York Times*. I was thrilled. It was the first time I had ever met him. I kept wondering if the side I was seeing was his real personality or the "Sanjeev Kapoor" that I saw on the show. It was a brief interview that left me longing for more.

I was in Mumbai recently and decided to call him to say hello. His friendly and very gentle wife called me back and invited me to their home for a home-cooked meal. A meal? At the home of THE Sanjeev Kapoor? My mom-in-law and my mother both, I think, had simultaneous coronaries when I told them. "Do you have any idea who he is? He is so big. He is amazing!" People always say you should never meet your idol. It breaks the magical spell. Well, I decided to do it anyway.

So with my six-month-old in my arms and my sister-in-law, who bribed me to let her come along, we went to Sanjeev's home in one of the most stylish and expensive areas of Mumbai. As we ascended the stairs of the villa, it seemed eerily quiet and I thought we had made a mistake and perhaps chosen the wrong day. But once the door opened, I knew we were in for a good time as a very welcoming family invited us in.

His wife seated us in their unpretentious yet elegantly appointed living room. Sanjeev appeared in a blue T-shirt and jeans, and was unfortunately fighting a severe nasal allergy. It is so silly but the first thought in my mind was—oh, even *he* gets colds! He sat with us and began to chat about movies and my trip and the baby as though we were long-lost friends. The same personality who had won so many over on TV was here, live and in person. One cannot fake that level of charm. My shy, stranger-averse baby went to Sanjeev and sat on his lap as his daughters played and made the baby laugh and giggle.

The appetizers began to show up. The one I remember with the most pleasure was the *golgappas* (small round flour balls) stuffed with shrimp sitting atop shot glasses filled with a lavender coconut curry. I picked one up tentatively. They were smashing. I began to laugh at myself. I had really set up in my mind that the afternoon would be terrible, that he would be a snob—based on the belief that all celebrities are snobs and full of themselves and that nothing would work out. I cannot even begin to tell you how wrong I was.

Sanjeev and his wife had gone out of their way and laid out a sumptuous meal for us—coconut-laced mutton curry, paneer sautéed with fresh bell peppers, a classic chicken curry—all food that they had cooked themselves. The most special dish Sanjeev prepared for us at the table, king-size prawns sautéed in mustard and red chiles.

He filled the afternoon with stories of rice that was eaten without cooking, of Bollywood hotshots and their eating habits, of being chased by fans and loving it. He showed me how to use his high-tech digital camera and laughed at the silly antics of my baby.

I broke the sacred rule—never meet your idol. And I am so glad I did.

It was one of the most enchanting afternoons I have ever spent. As we rode home, my sister-in-law called every single person she knew and began each conversation with, "Guess where I was for lunch?" ❋

Gulping Golgappas

The best way to serve these is to place each *golgappa* (turn to the next page for a better description) on a large table-spoon or preferably a Chinese soup spoon (Amazon sells a dozen for under five bucks). When your guests are ready for the shot, add your vodka of choice and have them put the whole golgappa, with the filling and the liquor in their mouth. It is messy, but that—along with the alcohol—is the best part!

I have used my favorite vodka flavors; feel free to substitute your own.

. . . .

1. Using your finger, gently poke a hole in each golgappa and fill it with ½ tablespoon of mashed potato and a pinch of cilantro. Place all of these on a plate.

2. When you are ready to serve the shots, place each golgappa on a spoon, pour in 2 tablespoons of one of the vodkas and eat/drink the whole thing in one gulp. (Eating it in one gulp is the key—otherwise it gets very messy!)

Chile Vodka

1 small green serrano chile, seeded and chopped
4 ounces (½ cup) plain vodka

In a tightly capped bottle, combine the chile and vodka. Allow it to sit for 10 minutes. Strain the vodka to remove the chile, then return the vodka to the bottle and chill for at least an hour.

Makes *40 pieces*
Prep/Cook time:
10 minutes (plus 15 minutes if you need to boil the potatoes)

40 store-bought golgappas
2 medium Idaho potatoes, boiled, peeled, mashed, and lightly salted
2 tablespoons minced cilantro
4 ounces (½ cup) Van Gogh Pomegranate Vodka, chilled
4 ounces (½ cup) Van Gogh Mango Vodka, chilled
4 ounces (½ cup) Van Gogh Coconut Vodka, chilled
4 ounces (½ cup) kaffir lime vodka such as Hangar One Kaffir Lime Vodka, chilled
4 ounces (½ cup) chile vodka, chilled (see recipe)

Hot Shots

Makes *20 shots*

Prep/Cook time:

20 minutes to make and

30 minutes to chill

For the Filling:

1 tablespoon vegetable oil

1 teaspoon black mustard
seeds

2 garlic cloves, minced

½ teaspoon red chile
powder or red chile
flakes

¼ teaspoon ground
turmeric

1 pound shrimp, peeled,
deveined, and diced

1 tablespoon fresh lemon
juice

Table salt

This recipe is dedicated to Chef Sanjeev Kapoor. Most Indian grocers now sell *golgappas*, also called *pani puris*, which are fried flour balloons. You poke a hole in the center of one and push a filling in. Golgappas are a popular street food in India; in this recipe they are served as a tapa.

If you cannot find golgappas, you can use the tortilla chips that look like small scoops. Both the filling and the cold soup can be made up to two days in advance. You will also need 20 shot glasses for this recipe.

So how do you eat these delights? Pop the golgappa in your mouth and then drink the soup (as you would eat a tapa with a glass of wine).

. . . .

To make the filling:

1. In a skillet, heat the oil over medium heat. When the oil begins to shimmer add the mustard seeds.

2. As the seeds begin to sizzle, add the garlic. Sauté for a few seconds, until the garlic begins to change color.

3. Add the red chile, turmeric, and shrimp, and cook for 2 minutes or just until the shrimp are no longer translucent. Do not overcook the shrimp or they will become rubbery.

4. Add the lemon juice and salt to taste. Mix well, remove from the heat, and set aside.

To make the soup:

5. In a small saucepan over medium-high heat, heat the oil until it shimmers and then add the asafetida (if using), mustard, cumin, and fenugreek seeds, and the curry leaves. Cook, stirring frequently, for a few seconds, until the seeds begin to splutter. Remove from heat and cool to room temperature.

6. Pour the buttermilk into a blender. Add the spice mixture, the garlic, turmeric, and salt.

7. Blend until the mixture is fairly smooth. There will be a few tiny pieces of curry leaves—this is fine.

8. Cover and refrigerate for at least 30 minutes or until cold.

To serve:

9. Pour 2 tablespoons of the soup into each shot glass. Fill each golgappa with about 2 teaspoons of the filling. Place a golgappa on top of a shot glass and serve.

For the Soup:

1 tablespoon vegetable oil

Pinch of asafetida (optional)

½ teaspoon black mustard seeds

½ teaspoon cumin seeds

⅛ teaspoon fenugreek seeds

10 fresh curry leaves

2 cups buttermilk

1 garlic clove, peeled

⅛ teaspoon ground turmeric

¼ teaspoon table salt

20 large store-bought golgappas

EMERALD-ADE

MAKES *3 cups, 6 servings*

PREP/COOK TIME:
*About 10 minutes hands-on,
45 minutes of unattended
cooking, and 3 hours to chill*

4 medium diced unpeeled
   green (unripe)
   mangoes (see Note)

7½ cups water

¼ cup superfine sugar

Pinch of black salt

2 tablespoons finely
   chopped fresh mint
   leaves

6 ounces (¾ cup) white
   rum

Ice as needed

This very mild, refreshing, almost ethereal drink is made with green mangoes. It is traditionally made in Northern India. I have seen and tasted several versions of it in which the mangoes are roasted in the oven, on an open flame, boiled, or even pressure-cooked before use. Each version has a different taste. I like this simple version that involves boiling the mango. The traditional recipe uses cumin, which I feel is overkill for this variation which has a very mild taste.

. . . .

1. Place the mangoes and water in a deep saucepan. Bring to a boil, reduce the heat, and simmer for about 45 minutes, until the mangoes have completely softened. Remove from the heat. With a potato masher, mash the mangoes gently to allow the pulp to flavor the water.

2. Allow the mixture to cool to room temperature. Strain the mango pulp from the water and discard the pulp. Reserve the water. (Reserve and add a bit of the mango pulp if you like a pulpy texture.)

3. Add the sugar, salt, and mint to the water. Mix well. Taste and adjust seasoning.

4. Chill for at least 3 hours.

5. Add the rum and mix once more.

6. Serve in tall ice-filled glasses.

Note: In this version of the drink, the skin of the mango is left on. If you want to make a pulpier version, peel the mangoes before dicing. Do not strain out the pulp. Allow the mixture to cool and then use a blender to blend the pulp and water into a smooth consistency.

CHAI ROCKS

SERVES *1*

PREP TIME: *5 minutes*

½ ounce (1 tablespoon)
  chilled vodka
1½ ounces (3 tablespoons)
  Voyant Chai Cream
  Liqueur
Pinch of ground
  cardamom
Ice as needed
Cinnamon stick

I had the good fortune to visit the Middle East recently. One of the modern Indian restaurants where I dined served an iced tea that was delightful, though a bit overdone with spices and alcohol. When I returned home, I experimented with it. Nothing seemed quite right until I found Voyant Chai Cream Liqueur—a wonderful liqueur made with rum, Indian black tea, and spices. I don't have a substitute for this, sorry!

• • • • • • • • • • • • • • •

Combine the vodka, Chai Cream, and cardamom in a cocktail shaker and shake well. Fill an old-fashioned glass with ice. Strain the drink into the glass. Add the cinnamon stick as a swizzle stick and serve.

LYCHEE-TINI

*L*ychee juice is a favorite alcohol-free summer drink in India. This recipe was developed after a great deal of experimenting. Lychees tend to be very sweet, and I needed to find a way to tame them. I tried lychee liquor and even the syrup in canned lychees, but found that nothing works better for this recipe than simple lychee juice.

You can use mango puree here instead of lychee juice for a mango-tini.

· · · · · · · · · · · · · · · ·

Combine the vodka, lychee juice, and lime juice in a cocktail shaker filled with ice cubes. Shake well. Place the lychee in a chilled martini glass and strain the drink over it. Place the ginger on the rim of the glass and serve.

SERVES *1*

PREP TIME: *5 minutes*

2 ounces (¼ cup) chilled vodka

2 ounces (¼ cup) chilled lychee juice such as Rubicon Lychee Juice

¼ ounce (½ tablespoon) sweetened lime juice such as Rose's

Ice as needed

1 fresh lychee, peeled

Small piece crystallized ginger for garnish

Serves *1*

Prep time: *5 minutes if you are using store-bought purees; if not, add time to make the purees*

Ice as needed

1½ ounces (3 tablespoons) chilled vodka

1½ ounces (3 tablespoons) mango puree (see page 41)

1½ ounces (3 tablespoons) papaya puree (see recipe)

4 ounces (½ cup) chilled ginger ale

Fresh mint leaves for garnish

This recipe takes the mango off the plate and into the glass, and does so in a unique and sophisticated way. Mango puree, usually sweetened, is available from most Indian grocers. You can substitute any rich fruit puree here.

. . . .

Fill a tall glass, like a collins glass, with ice. Add the vodka, mango puree, papaya puree, and ginger ale and stir well. Serve garnished with mint leaves.

To prepare papaya puree: Peel the papaya, cut in half, and remove the black seeds inside. Dice into small pieces. Place in a blender and puree to a smooth paste. Always select a fully ripe papaya for this. You can add a touch of sugar, if needed, for extra sweetness.

Note: If you are making fruit purees at home, be sure to blend them well and then strain them to make sure they don't have any clumps or fibers.

Tamarita

I've loved tamarind since I was a kid and ate the raw green ones in pods. As an adult, one of my favorite ways to enjoy it is as part of a drink. This recipe shows off a great flavor combination: tamarind with tequila. Chef K. N. Vinod, who owns Indique Heights in Chevy Chase, Maryland, shared his recipe with me several years ago and it gives me great pleasure to share it with you here.

. . . .

Fill a tall glass such as a collins glass with ice. Add the tequila, triple sec, chutney, and sour mix. Stir well. Serve garnished with a lemon wedge.

Note: Please do not use tamarind extract, tamarind paste, or fresh tamarind juice in this recipe; it will not give you the right taste. The tamarind-date chutney has just the right mix of sugar and spice to really play up the taste of tamarind.

SERVES *1*

PREP TIME: *5 minutes*

Ice as needed

1½ ounces (3 tablespoons) tequila (such as Cuervo Gold)

1 ounce (2 tablespoons) triple sec

½ ounce (1 tablespoon) store-bought tamarind-date chutney (see Note)

1½ ounces (3 tablespoons) sour mix

Lemon wedge for garnish

TROPICAL SUNSET

SERVES *1*

PREP TIME: *5 minutes*

Ice as needed

¾ ounce (1½ tablespoons)
   coconut rum (such as
   Malibu)

¾ ounce (1½ tablespoons)
   pineapple rum (such as
   Malibu)

4 ounces (½ cup) guava
   juice (such as Rubicon
   Guava Juice)

This recipe marries all my favorite childhood flavors—guava, pineapple, and coconut—to create a perfect tropical drink.

. . . .

Fill a tall glass such as a collins glass with ice. Add the rums and guava juice. Stir well and serve.

TANGY TRACK

Rum is one of the most popular drinks in India. During my college years, I remember rum and Coke being the preferred ultra-easy cocktail of choice for most party-goers. More complex cocktails are very popular now as tastes are changing. As you play with this drink, try adding a touch of pineapple juice for a tasty variation.

. . . .

Fill a tall glass such as a collins glass with ice. Add the rum, orange juice, lime juice, and bitters and stir well. Serve garnished with an orange slice.

SERVES *1*
PREP TIME: *5 minutes*

Ice as needed
1½ ounces (3 tablespoons) coconut rum such as Malibu
2 ounces (¼ cup) orange juice
¼ ounce (½ tablespoon) sweetened lime juice such as Rose's
Splash of orange bitters
Orange slice for garnish

HOT PASSION

SERVES *1*

PREP TIME: *5 minutes*

Ice as needed

1½ ounces (3 tablespoons)
pineapple rum

4 ounces (½ cup)
pineapple juice

¼ ounce (½ tablespoon)
sweetened lime juice
such as Rose's

2 small green serrano
chiles, slit and gently
pounded using a
mortar and pestle

Green chiles are generally used in cooking and rarely seen in drinks in India. I love to add them to my rum! If you are worried about the heat, don't pound them; simply swirl a slit green serrano chile in the drink just before serving. You can also substitute jalapeños for the hot green chiles in this recipe.

. . . .

Fill a tall glass such as a collins glass with ice. Add the rum, pineapple juice, lime juice, and chiles. Stir well and serve.

RUM AND ROSES

I make this drink with a traditional syrup called Rooh Afza. Hamdard, the company that makes the syrup, says on its website, "Rooh Afza—one that enhances the spirit and uplifts the soul." It lends a gorgeous pink color to this drink. There is no substitute for Rooh Afza.

The rose petals you use for this recipe should be pesticide free. Edible flowers are specifically marked so please be sure to use the correct roses.

. . . .

Mix the rose syrup, lime juice, and rum in a tall glass. Fill the glass with ice and add the club soda. Stir gently, garnish with rose petals, and serve.

SERVES *1*

PREP TIME: 5 *minutes*

1 tablespoon Rooh Afza
½ teaspoon sweetened lime juice such as Rose's
1½ ounces (3 tablespoons) white rum
Ice as needed
4 ounces (½ cup) chilled club soda
Rose petals for garnish

POMEGRANATE DELIGHT

SERVES *1*

PREP TIME: *5 minutes*

¼ ounce (½ tablespoon)
grenadine

½ ounce (1 tablespoon)
store-bought
pomegranate juice (see
Note)

½ teaspoon sweetened
lime juice such as
Rose's

1½ ounces (3 tablespoons)
white rum

Ice as needed

4 ounces (½ cup) chilled
club soda

This drink is a gorgeous deep burgundy. You can use pomegranate liqueur too, if you like—add ¼ ounce (½ tablespoon).

. . . .

Mix the grenadine, pomegranate juice, lime juice, and rum in a tall glass. Add ice and the club soda and stir gently. Serve immediately.

Note: You can use plain POM pomegranate juice for this recipe, or try one of the mixed varieties such as Pomegranate-Blueberry for an exotic-tasting cocktail.

GUAVA BELLINI

Sip Champagne with a touch of the exotic. This refreshing and classy cocktail is one of the most popular drinks in our house during summer. If you cannot find guava puree, you can use guava juice.

. . . .

Gently mix the puree and ginger juice in a Champagne flute. Slowly add the Champagne. Stir gently. Garnish with raspberries and serve.

Note: To make ginger juice, grate fresh ginger using a cheese grater, then use your fingers to squeeze the juice from the pulp. Discard the grated ginger pulp.

SERVES *1*
PREP TIME: *10 minutes*

2 tablespoons pink guava puree (see page 246)
1 teaspoon ginger juice (see Note)
4 to 6 ounces chilled Champagne or dry sparkling wine
Fresh cold raspberries for garnish

Mismatched Matches

Yesterday morning my husband of fifteen years, Sameer, and I had one of the worst arguments of our married life. We are civil arguers: We don't yell and scream or hurl accusations. We discuss, we debate and declare. And yesterday we declared that we clearly did not understand each other and were totally mismatched. He diets, I write cookbooks; he loves *Die Hard,* I want to live near the bridge in Madison County; he loves music and plays instruments, I could not recognize a note if it slammed me over the head; we are the epitome of "as different as chalk and cheese."

He stormed out of the kitchen in a huff and I sat there seething. The specifics of our argument are not relevant so I won't mention them, but suffice it to say that we were both *really* angry.

His way of dealing with conflict is to go running; I am an indoor person and my way is to fix/change/cook/decorate/redecorate something in the kitchen. He left the house to run and after stomping around the house for a bit, I finally decided I was going to "fix" our collection of coffee and teacups. Nothing matched and there were even cracks in some of the cups. How could we live like this? Ah. The shame of it all, what did our friends think when I, a food writer and cookbook author, served them coffee or tea in mismatched cups? Pathetic, really.

I began by laying out the entire collection of fifteen mismatched cups on the table. I also found, hidden way behind the cups, a totally unused English Rose pattern tea set.

I decided to sell some of the old cups on eBay. Aficionados of eBay swear that pictures are great sales tools, so after hand-washing each cup, I laid them on the table to take pictures. Quickly, I uploaded all the shots and then began the task of writing descriptions.

First up, an old ceramic coffee cup with CNN printed on the front. We had purchased it about eleven years ago, at the CNN studio in Atlanta. Hand in hand we had toured the studio for an hour. Initially, my husband did not want to go to Atlanta, but I had always dreamed of being a reporter and so he had arranged this trip for me. It was how we began our delayed honeymoon. Could I part with this?

The next cup was part of a chipped set—beautiful blue flowers painted onto a bone china cup with a matching teapot. It was given to us as a gift about eight years ago by friends who became our son's godparents. Sameer and I had toasted in this set the day we had brought our baby home—he had ginger tea and I had coffee. We had laughed and cried and wondered what we would do with this brand-new life we had just created and whether we were even worthy of such a wonderful blessing. Finally we had decided to save these cups and give them to our son when he was older. Okay, I could not sell these. So back in the cabinet they went.

The next set were four pedestaled cups I had bought at Target, thirteen years ago. A young bride then, I was trying to prove to my frugal husband that I knew how to hunt for bargains and was not a wasteful spender. He had taught me, a coffee drinker, how to make tea:

the exact point at which to add the tea leaves to the boiling water, how long to simmer until the amber hue was just right, how to grate the ginger (using a cheese grater, no less), and to add it toward the end so it could release all its earthy goodness. And finally to add a few tablespoons of milk and quite a bit of sugar to get it just sweet enough. I practiced for years to perfect it to his taste and of course always served it in my simple pedestaled Target cups. They were a dollar fifty each. But they had an expensive look about them and I stored them in my china cabinet along with all our wedding crystal. Last year, the cabinet fell and I lost everything except these cups. My husband spent hours consoling me, calling my Target cups "the survivors." Yes, back in the cabinet they went.

The next set showcased Sameer's love for collecting cups from all the places we had worked—five in all. I hated these big mugs; they did not match and I disliked serving guests with promotional mugs. Yet each one reflected a time in our life—a few years with a Big Six consulting firm in Cleveland; two hard years with a start-up in Boston, and now a blessed life with a software company in Washington, D.C. They were, in a way, milestones of sorts. So far, I was selling nothing. Finally I turned to the unused set of English Rose tea-cups with matching saucers. Even though Sameer hated shopping, he had given these to me for our first anniversary. I had never used them. I kept saving them for the "right time" with the "right people," and for the perfect occasion.

I heard the door open. Sameer was back from his run. He stopped by the breakfast table where I had spread the teacups.

"Are you okay?" he asked and then, glancing at the English Rose cups, "are we expecting company?"

"I am fine," I replied, "No company, I was just cleaning up."

"Good," he smiled gently. "After my shower, can you make me some ginger tea?"

I made his tea and my coffee and served it in our English Rose tea set: a matching-cup toast to mismatches made in heaven. ☀

GINGER TEA

1. In a saucepan, bring the water to a boil. Add the tea leaves and ginger.

2. Add the milk and remove from the heat. Allow to steep for a minute or two.

3. Strain. Add sugar to taste and serve in your best teacups.

Note: Please use freshly grated ginger for this recipe. The store-bought stuff won't do it—and also no ginger powder. The pungency of the freshly grated ginger is what gives this tea its taste.

SERVES 2
PREP TIME: *10 minutes*

1½ cups water
1 tablespoon loose Indian
  tea leaves
¼ teaspoon grated fresh
  ginger (see Note)
½ cup milk
Sugar to taste

GUAVA-PAPAYA SMOOTHIE

SERVES *2*

PREP TIME: *5 minutes*

½ cup pink guava puree
  (see page 246)
¾ cup papaya puree (see
  page 62)
¼ cup coconut milk
Ice as needed (1 cup to
  start)

This is a great summer drink, and also a fantastic breakfast drink. You can punch it up with some dark rum for an exciting evening cocktail.

. . . .

Place all the ingredients in a blender and blend until smooth. Pour into tall glasses and serve immediately.

APPETIZERS, SNACKS, and SALADS

....

Purists maintain that traditional Indian food is not composed of courses, as in the European model. While in India meals are always served as a single course with salads, entrees, sides, breads, rice, and sometimes even dessert presented together, I have yet to eat in a single Indian home or restaurant or attend any Indian food-related occasion where appetizers were not served! When I was growing up, my mother would serve traditional, single course meals for the family. But when she was entertaining, appetizers were certain to show up on the menu. In recent years, I have eaten many dinners at the homes of dear Indian friends that consisted solely of hearty appetizers and drinks with nothing that could be called a main course. Personally, I really love this fun concept and have thrown many such parties myself.

Snacking is a time-honored Indian tradition. Yes, Indians do love to snack, and snack time is literally anytime tea is served. Snacks can require elaborate preparation, like the samosa, or be as simple as a fish fry or an even simpler bowl of trail-mix-style snack called *chivda*. No teatime is complete without munchies. Many of these same snacks have made their way onto the appetizer lists of Indian restaurants and home cooks. Desserts are also a large part of snacking—nothing like a *gulab jamun* (milk dumplings in a sugary syrup) to help a cup of tea go down even more smoothly!

Salads, too, were not served separately in traditional Indian cuisine. However, as tastes change, I find more and more that I and many of my friends are incorporating salads in our menus as entrees. Some of the traditional Indian yogurt salads that provide cooling effects when served with a spicy meal, I now find myself serving as appetizers or sides to a meal.

In this chapter, I am presenting you with fun, new recipes for appetizers or snacks (whatever you wish to call them) and salads. The recipes are easy to prepare and delightful to share with friends. You can pair them with cocktails from the Modern Drinks chapter of this book.

Peanut Tikkis
with Tamarind-Date Chutney

Okay, these *tikkis* (patties) take practice to make perfectly. Make sure the peanuts are not ground to a fine powder; there should be small pieces in the mix. Pan-fry over medium heat to make them perfectly crunchy outside and moist on the inside.

. . . .

1. Boil the potatoes, peel, and mash them. Mix in bell pepper, bread crumbs, corn, pomegranate seeds (if using), salt, chile powder, cilantro, and peanuts. (Watch your salt here, since the peanuts are already salted.)

2. Divide the mixture into 10 equal portions. Grease or wet your hands, take a portion, roll it into a ball, then flatten it into a small round patty, or tikki. Repeat with the remaining mixture.

3. Heat the oil in a medium skillet over medium heat. When the oil begins to shimmer, add as many patties as you can without crowding the pan.

4. Fry for 1 to 2 minutes on each side, until golden brown. Remove the cooked tikki from the skillet and place on paper towels to drain. Continue until all the tikkis are cooked.

5. Serve hot, topped with the chutney. (You can keep these warm in a low oven.)

Note: Japanese panko are very fluffy bread crumbs used to create a crunchy coating for fried dishes. They do so without giving a very "bready" or heavy taste since the panko crumbs are made with just the bread and not the bread crusts. If you don't have panko, you can use regular dry bread crumbs, although I would recommend trying to get panko—you won't regret it!

MAKES *10 patties*
PREP/COOK TIME:
40 minutes

2 medium Idaho potatoes, scrubbed

¼ cup finely diced red bell pepper

¼ cup fine bread crumbs such as Japanese panko (see Note)

½ cup cooked corn kernels

¼ cup fresh pomegranate seeds (optional)

¼ teaspoon table salt to start

1 teaspoon red chile powder or red chile flakes

1 tablespoon minced cilantro

½ cup roasted, salted peanuts, coarsely ground

6 tablespoons vegetable oil

Store-bought tamarind-date chutney for drizzling

MASALA OMELET WITH GREEN CHILE CHUTNEY

MAKES *60 small pieces*

PREP/COOK TIME:

20 minutes

6 medium eggs

¼ small red onion, finely
   diced

¼ teaspoon ground
   turmeric

¼ teaspoon table salt

½ teaspoon red chile
   powder or red chile
   flakes

1 tablespoon finely
   minced cilantro

2 tablespoons vegetable
   oil

60 crispy pastry shells
   (1½-inch wide and ½-
   inch deep) such as
   Siljans Croustades

5 tablespoons store-
   bought or homemade
   Green Chile Chutney
   (recipe opposite)

When I was growing up, my father would make these delicious omelets as a snack. You can top them with warmed sesame seeds, if you like, or even with finely diced bell peppers in various colors.

· · · · · · · · · · · · · · ·

1. In a bowl, whisk the eggs to blend. Whisk in the onions, turmeric, salt, chile powder, and the cilantro.

2. In a medium nonstick skillet, heat about 1 tablespoon of the vegetable oil over medium heat. Pour about ½ the egg mixture and cook until the underside is golden brown. Flip over and cook the other side until the omelet is firm and cooked through. Transfer to a plate. Repeat for the remaining oil and egg mixture.

3. Allow the omelets to cool for about 10 minutes. Using your hands, break the omelets into very small pieces. You can use a fork and knife to cut them up if you like but nothing works like your hands.

4. Divide evenly among the pastry shells, top each with ¼ teaspoon of the green chile chutney and serve immediately.

GREEN CHILE CHUTNEY

Combine the cilantro, chiles, lemon juice, and garlic in a blender. Add a little water to aid in blending and blend until smooth. Transfer to a container, stir in salt to taste, cover, and refrigerate until needed. This will keep for 3 to 4 days, covered, in the refrigerator.

Did you know . . . that the *Arabian Nights* mentions cilantro as an aphrodisiac?

MAKES *about 1 cup*
PREP TIME: *10 minutes*

2 cups cilantro (leaves and tender stems)
20 medium green serrano chiles
2 tablespoons fresh lemon juice
2 garlic cloves, peeled
Salt

PANEER WITH ORANGE-APRICOT CHUTNEY

MAKES *54 pieces paneer and about* 1¾ *to* 2 *cups chutney*

PREP/COOK TIME: *45 minutes*

FOR THE PANEER:

400-gram/14-ounce paneer slab

1½ tablespoons vegetable oil

FOR THE CHUTNEY:

1 tablespoon vegetable oil

1 teaspoon black mustard seeds (see Note)

4 to 6 fresh apricots, pitted and diced (about 1½ cups)

1 tablespoon minced, peeled fresh ginger

1 small green serrano chile, seeded and minced

2 cups fresh orange juice

2 tablespoons fresh lemon juice

This is a simple and delicious appetizer. Slabs of paneer, an Indian cheese, are slathered with warmed orange-apricot chutney. I usually allow for four cubes per guest. This is a great appetizer for a large crowd. I strongly suggest using fresh apricots for this if you can find them—canned ones just melt into the chutney and dried ones don't provide the same texture. If you cannot find apricots, use 1½ cups diced fresh mangoes instead.

. . . .

1. Cut the paneer into six slabs, 2½ by 2 inches by ¼-inch thick. Heat the oil in a large skillet over medium-high heat. Add the paneer slabs. Cook for about 2 minutes on each side, until the paneer is well browned. It should be a medium-golden brown color. Don't overcook, as it will make the paneer rubbery. Remove from the heat and drain on a paper towel.

2. While the paneer rests, prepare the chutney. Heat the oil in a deep saucepan over medium heat. When it begins to shimmer, add the mustard seeds and cook for about 30 seconds, until they begin to sizzle.

3. Add the apricots, ginger, chile, orange and lemon juices, chile powder, saffron, sugar, and dates. Mix well. Cook over medium heat for about 25 minutes, until the chutney has thickened and the apricots have mostly dissolved. There will be a few pieces left.

4. Remove from the heat and stir in salt to taste.

5. Cut each slab of paneer into nine cubes. Place the warm chutney in an attractive bowl in the center of a platter. Sur-

round with the cubed paneer. Add toothpicks to the paneer pieces and serve.

$\mathcal{D}$id you know . . . black mustard seeds are at the center of much Indian folklore. My grandmother used to tell me to spread mustard seeds at the entrance of the house. She said it kept the witches away because they spent time counting the tiny seeds! In rural India, a teaspoon of mustard seeds waved over the heads of children is also supposed to ward off the evil eye!

$\mathcal{N}$ote: Mustard seeds burn easily so keep an eye on them when they are cooking. They also tend to sputter and spew as if they are angry and want to make their presence felt. So watch yourself when you cook them! There is no saving burnt mustard seeds; discard them and start again.

1 teaspoon red chile powder or red chile flakes
Pinch of saffron
2 tablespoons sugar
¼ cup chopped dates such as Dole's chopped dates
Table salt

CHILE PEA PUFFS

MAKES *32 puffs*

PREP/COOK TIME:

35 minutes

Nonstick cooking spray
1 cup cooked green peas,
    preferably petit peas,
    lightly mashed
¼ cup crumbled paneer
2 small green serrano
    chiles, minced (remove
    the seeds before
    mincing if you want to
    reduce the heat)
¼ teaspoon table salt to
    start
¼ teaspoon red chile
    powder or red chile
    flakes (less if you don't
    like the heat)
½ teaspoon minced garlic
32 wonton wrappers
1 egg white, lightly
    beaten

I love using prepared wonton skins for simple party appetizers. They taste great and give the impression that you have spent hours slaving away in the kitchen! While I do realize that wonton skins are not used in the traditional Indian kitchen, several friends in India and here in the United States now use them regularly for dishes similar to this one.

I prefer baking these puffs. If you decide to deep-fry them, remember that the key to getting a good puff is to maintain the temperature of the oil between batches. Drop a tiny piece of bread or a small piece of the wonton skin into the hot oil; if it rises immediately to the top, the oil is ready to be used. Never reuse oil that has been used for deep-frying.

Serve these with Kumquat and Mango Chutney with Onion Seeds (page 41) or Mint-Cilantro Chutney (page 36).

. . . .

1. Preheat the oven to 400°F. Lightly grease a baking sheet with cooking spray.

2. In a bowl combine the peas, paneer, green chiles, salt, chile powder, and garlic. Mix well.

3. Place 1 teaspoon of the mixture into a center of a wonton wrapper. Lightly brush the edges of the wrapper with the egg white. Fold the wrapper over to form a triangle, or if you are using round wrappers, fold to form a half-moon. Press the edges with a fork, gently, to secure the seam so the filling does not fall out.

4. Place the puffs in a single layer on the baking sheet. Spray them lightly with cooking spray.

5. Cook for 7 to 8 minutes or until they are crisp and the skin changes to a lovely golden brown. Turn once, halfway through baking.

6. Serve immediately with your choice of chutney.

CRAB TIKKIS

MAKES *6 to 8 cakes*
PREP/COOK TIME:
20 minutes plus 30 minutes
refrigeration time

½ pound jumbo lump
  crabmeat, such as
  Phillips brand, picked
  over
2 small shallots, finely
  chopped
1 small green serrano
  chile, finely chopped
1 teaspoon minced peeled
  fresh ginger (see Note)
1 teaspoon cumin seeds
1 tablespoon finely
  chopped cilantro
1 medium egg
6 tablespoons fine bread
  crumbs such as
  Japanese panko,
  divided
½ teaspoon table salt
2 tablespoons vegetable
  oil
Store-bought tamarind-
  date chutney for
  garnish

*L*uscious crab combined with traditional Indian spices cre-
ates a unique crab cake in this recipe. Garlic and cumin
flavor these mini crab cakes, which I serve drizzled with tamarind-date chutney. You can also prepare salmon tikkis the same
way; use flaked raw salmon instead of crab, but be sure to adjust
the cooking time. Cook until salmon is no longer pink and is
cooked through.

. . . .

1. In a bowl combine the crab, shallots, chile, ginger, cumin, cilantro, egg, 4 tablespoons of the bread crumbs, and the salt. Mix
well.

2. Divide the mixture into 6 or 8 portions and use your hands to
shape each portion into a small ball.

3. Flatten each ball into a patty about 1 inch thick. These will be
loosely held patties. (If you are having trouble with them staying
bound, add a tablespoon more of the bread crumbs.) Dredge the
patties with the remaining crumbs.

4. Arrange on a sheet pan, cover with plastic wrap, and refrigerate for about 30 minutes. If a patty falls apart, gently pat it together again.

5. Heat a large skillet and add 1 tablespoon of the oil. Place half
the patties in the oil and cook over medium heat 3 to 4 minutes
on each side until the outside is crispy and brown. Add another
tablespoon of oil and cook the remaining patties. Place cooked
patties in a 200°F oven to keep warm if needed.

6. Serve drizzled with tamarind-date chutney.

Note: Mincing ginger, particularly in small quantities, is tricky if you don't know how to do it. One option is of course to buy the minced ginger in a jar! A fresher option is to peel it and use a small hand-held cheese grater to grate the ginger. It works well and saves you from cleaning up a large food processor for one small piece of ginger.

GARAM MASALA CHICKEN

MAKES *30 pieces*

PREP/COOK TIME: *50 minutes*

2 pounds bone-in, skin-on chicken breasts

½ small red onion, sliced

4 garlic cloves, peeled

1 small cinnamon stick

1 bay leaf

2 black cardamom pods

2 cups low-sodium chicken broth

2 tablespoons vegetable oil

1 teaspoon cumin seeds

1-inch piece fresh ginger, peeled and grated

1 small red onion, pureed

2 small tomatoes, peeled and pureed

¼ teaspoon table salt to start

½ teaspoon red chile powder or red chile flakes

My mom often refers to this dish as "Mona's chili chicken"——Mona being her special name for me. I use whole (not ground) warming spices—the garam masala—when poaching the chicken. They give the chicken a wonderful base. While I use a simple poaching method to cook the chicken, you can use plain grilled chicken or leftover rotisserie chicken for this recipe as well. Just make sure that it is not already seasoned.

Please don't let this long list of ingredients scare you off——the whole spices like cinnamon and bay leaf are used to flavor the chicken. If you don't want to use so many spices, just use the cinnamon stick to start with. The next time you prepare the recipe, add a few more of the whole spices and see how the flavor gets richer and develops more layers.

. . . .

1. In a deep saucepan, combine the chicken, sliced onion, garlic, cinnamon, bay leaf, cardamom, and chicken broth. Bring to a boil, reduce the heat to a low simmer, cover, and cook until the chicken is cooked through, about 30 minutes.

2. Remove the chicken from the broth and allow to cool to room temperature. Discard the bones and skin. Shred the chicken into bite-sized pieces using your fingers or a fork. (Strain the broth and reserve for future use such as cooking white basmati rice.)

3. Heat the vegetable oil in a large skillet over medium heat. When the oil begins to shimmer, add the cumin seeds. In a few seconds the seeds will begin to sizzle. Add the ginger and pureed onion and cook for 4 to 5 minutes, until the onion just begins to change color.

4. Add the tomatoes, salt, chile powder, turmeric, coriander, and cilantro. Mix well and cook for another 5 to 7 minutes, until oil begins to separate from the sides of the mixture.

5. Add the chicken and cook for another 2 to 3 minutes, until all the flavors have blended well together. Remove from heat. (This mixture can be prepared a couple of days in advance and reheated just before serving.)

6. Heap a generous tablespoon of the mixture on each of the bread slices and serve immediately.

Did you know . . . black cardamom pods provide fragrance and flavor but, like cinnamon sticks, they are not edible so remove before serving! They provide a deep, smoky flavor to dishes. They are not eaten raw.

¼ teaspoon ground turmeric

2 teaspoons ground coriander

2 tablespoons minced cilantro

30 slices Italian bread (2 loaves cut into fifteen ¾- to 1-inch thick slices each)

GINGER SHRIMP

SERVES *6 to 8*

PREP/COOK TIME:
*10 minutes plus 30 minutes
for refrigeration*

2 teaspoons grated peeled
   fresh ginger
½ teaspoon red chile
   powder or red chile
   flakes
¼ teaspoon ground
   turmeric
½ teaspoon carom seeds
¼ teaspoon table salt to
   start
1 pound jumbo shrimp
   (26 to 30 per pound),
   peeled and deveined,
   thawed if frozen (see
   Note)
1 tablespoon vegetable oil
Fresh lemon juice for
   garnish

I like using jumbo shrimp for this pleasing appetizer. I don't generally serve it with a dipping sauce since it doesn't need any embellishments. My family, however, is chutney obsessed and will always look at me with a "Where is the dip for this?" expression. So I give in and serve it with a cilantro (page 36) or hot chile chutney (page 79).

Shrimp are best served as soon as they are cooked, so this is not a do-ahead dish. If you have any leftover shrimp, cut them up and toss them with cooked basmati rice for a simple pilaf.

. . . .

1. Combine the ginger, chile powder, turmeric, carom seeds, salt, and shrimp in a large mixing bowl. Toss to thoroughly combine. Make sure the shrimp are well coated. Refrigerate, covered, for at least 30 minutes.

2. Heat the vegetable oil in a large skillet over high heat. When the oil begins to shimmer, add the shrimp mixture. Cook for 1 minute. Reduce the heat to medium and cook, stirring often, 3 to 4 minutes, until the shrimp are opaque. (Shrimp cook very quickly.)

3. Serve immediately with a sprinkle of lemon juice.

Note: The best way to thaw frozen shrimp is under cold running water, not in hot water or the microwave.

Achari Chicken Salad

Achari means pickled. This filling salad is tangy and spicy. I use store-bought mango pickle, puree it, and use it as a marinade. You can vary this dish by trying out the different types of pickles from the market. Remove any hard pits or other hard ingredients that won't be easily pureed. I like to serve this chicken by itself or over baby spinach; you can also serve it over plain couscous.

. . . .

1. Place the pickle in a small nonreactive bowl. Using the back of a metal tablespoon, press down on the pickle to find and remove any hard pieces that cannot be pureed. Scrape the pickle into a mini food processor. Add the water and mix well. Blend to a smooth puree.

2. Transfer the pureed pickle to a medium bowl and add the ginger-garlic paste, turmeric, salt, and cooking oil. Mix well. Add the chicken to the marinade and stir to coat all the pieces. Refrigerate, covered, until needed.

3. Preheat the oven to 400°F.

4. Line a roasting pan with foil and grease it lightly with nonstick cooking spray. Place the chicken in a single layer on the foil and pour any remaining marinade on top of the chicken.

5. Bake for 20 to 25 minutes, until the chicken is cooked through and the juices run clear.

6. Arrange the spinach and onion on a large platter. Top with the chicken and serve immediately.

SERVES 4
PREP/COOK TIME: 45 minutes

2 tablespoons store-bought mango pickle such as Ruchi Mango Avakkai Pickle
2 tablespoons water
2 teaspoons store-bought ginger-garlic paste
¼ teaspoon ground turmeric
¼ teaspoon table salt
2 tablespoons cooking oil
1 pound skinless boneless chicken cut into 2-inch chunks (or chicken tenders)
Nonstick cooking spray
2 cups lightly packed baby spinach, washed and dried
½ small red onion, peeled and thinly sliced

TADKA SOUP WITH CRAB

MAKES *4 small or 2 large servings*

PREP/COOK TIME: *35 minutes*

2 tablespoons unsalted butter

2 garlic cloves, peeled and chopped

1 small yellow onion, peeled and thinly sliced

One 15.5-ounce can cannellini beans, drained and rinsed

2 cups chicken broth

¼ cup heavy cream

Table salt and ground white pepper

¼ pound cooked lump crab such as Phillips brand, picked over

1 tablespoon ghee or cooking oil

¼ teaspoon deghi mirch (see Note)

⅛ teaspoon red chile flakes

Traditional soups in India are made with lentils (or beans), onions, tomatoes, and a large array of spices, and then topped with a tempering of another array of spices. *Tadka* means tempering, and tempering means heating oil and adding spices to it. Spices release their flavors to the hot oil. While lentil-based soups are rewarding in taste, they are too time-consuming for our family for weeknights since most lentils take a long time to cook. When I discovered canned cannellini beans, I knew I had a solution. When I first served this soup to my mom, she tasted it grudgingly—cannellini beans are not something she is familiar with. But she had to admit, it was love at first sip, especially since the flaming red of the *deghi mirch* (a red chile that provides color but not heat) and the smell of the clarified butter made it taste like home!

. . . .

1. Melt the butter in a medium skillet over medium heat. Add the garlic and onion. Sauté for about 10 minutes, or until transparent and soft.

2. Add the beans and cook another 5 minutes.

3. Add the broth and simmer for 15 minutes.

4. Remove from the heat and allow to come to room temperature. Puree in a blender until smooth. (If you prefer a really smooth soup, pass the puree through a strainer.)

5. Add the heavy cream. Check the seasoning and adjust as necessary with salt and pepper.

6. Reheat the soup to a gentle simmer.

7. Ladle the soup into serving bowls and top each with an equal amount of crab.

8. In a small saucepan (or skillet), heat the ghee or oil over medium heat. Add the deghi mirch and chile flakes. Remove from the heat immediately and drizzle over the soup. Serve warm.

Note: Deghi mirch is the Indian version of paprika. MDH brand sells a good product. If you don't have this, use paprika instead. It is mild and adds color without adding a lot of heat.

SERVES *4*

PREP/COOK TIME: *10*

minutes

Nonstick cooking spray

Juice of 1 lemon

**¼ cup warmed liquid
    honey**

**8 fresh figs, stemmed,
    trimmed and halved**

8 pitted dried dates

**Store-bought chaat
    masala to sprinkle over
    finished dish**

HAVE A DATE WITH A FIG

Armed with every piece of formal clothing I owned, I attended a week-long, fifteen-event wedding in Delhi, on November 23, 2003, when 28,000 brides and grooms tied the knot. (November 23 was a day marked as auspicious by local priests.) The wedding celebrations included all three meals a day for hundreds of guests and their entourages of servants and chauffeurs. Each meal in itself was an event. Chefs and cooks were ferried in from various parts of old Delhi and other Indian cities along with their mobile kitchens, *haandis* (cooking vessels), enormous *tandoors* (clay ovens), and troops of helpers.

On the third day of the wedding, at an outdoor event with 500 guests and thirty folk dancers, the food reflected updated tandoori cooking. That evening it was cold and rows of tandoor ovens lined the sides of the large pavilion giving off their warmth. The longest line was for an old cook serving fresh figs and dates on long metal skewers, freshly grilled in the tandoor. The sweetness of the figs, intensified by the heat of the oven, was set off by the tanginess of the lemon and the chaat masala.

Since we don't have tandoor ovens in our homes, I have modified this recipe so you can enjoy it. Use fresh figs if they are available, but the recipe will also work with dried figs if you shorten the cooking time so they are just heated through. You must try this recipe! This will taste like fig-date sweet and savory candy!

. . . .

1. Preheat the broiler. Spray a baking sheet with a gentle mist of nonstick cooking spray.

2. Place the lemon juice and honey in a bowl and mix very well. Add the figs and dates and toss to thoroughly coat the fruit.

3. Place the figs and dates on the prepared baking sheet and pour any remaining liquid on top of the fruits. Place under the broiler at least 3 inches from the heat. The figs and dates take only a minute or two on each side; they may char a little, and the liquid will begin to caramelize.

4. Remove the baking sheet from under the boiler and use tongs to transfer the fruit to a small plate.

5. Sprinkle sparingly with the chaat masala and serve hot.

Alternately, you can arrange the figs and dates on skewers and grill them over medium-hot charcoal. Watch carefully, as they can burn quickly.

Did you know . . . we call them fruits, but figs are actually inverted flowers?

HEIRLOOM TOMATO SALAD WITH CHAAT MASALA

SERVES *4*

PREP TIME: *10 minutes*

2 pounds assorted
heirloom tomatoes
2 tablespoons fresh lemon
juice
Store-bought chaat
masala
10 to 20 fresh basil leaves,
shredded

Summer tomatoes taste best when very little is done to them—they are already so fresh and full of flavor. Use different sizes and colors of tomatoes for this recipe. Let the salad sit for at least 20 minutes before you serve it to allow the flavors to meld.

I don't use any vinegar or garlic here, and I promise you will not miss it—the fruity taste of the tomatoes is perfectly balanced by the tart, salty taste of the chaat masala. When I make this in India, I use *tulsi* (Indian basil). It is almost impossible to find here so I substitute regular American basil.

. . . .

1. Slice the tomatoes. Arrange the slices attractively on a serving platter.

2. Pour the lemon juice over the tomatoes and sprinkle with chaat masala to taste. Allow to sit for 20 minutes. Garnish with the basil leaves and serve.

CILANTRO-LEMON CORN POPS

$\mathcal{N}$ecessity is the mother of invention—or should I say pregnancy is! During my first pregnancy I craved popcorn. But I did not want it just salty (and definitely did not want it sweet)—I wanted it spicy and I wanted it laced with the fresh ingredients I loved like cilantro and red onions. So before my first son was born, a new recipe came into the world that combined my love of spices and popcorn. This dish is meant to be eaten as soon as it is prepared, as the popcorn will get soggy if you keep it too long. Enjoy it with a cold, cold iced tea as you watch your favorite movie.

. . . .

1. In a deep lidded saucepan, heat the oil. As soon as it shimmers add the cumin, chile powder, turmeric, and salt. Add the corn kernels and stir to mix well.

2. Partially cover the pan, leaving a small gap for the steam to escape. Shake the pan a few times during the cooking process. Cook until the kernels have stopped popping. This should take 4 to 5 minutes.

3. Remove from the heat. Add the onion, lemon juice, cilantro, and peanuts. Mix well and serve immediately.

MAKES *3 quarts*
PREP/COOK TIME: *10 minutes*

3 tablespoons vegetable oil
½ teaspoon ground cumin (see Note)
½ teaspoon red chile powder
¼ teaspoon ground turmeric
¼ teaspoon table salt to start
½ cup popping corn kernels
½ small red onion, diced
1½ tablespoons fresh lemon juice
1 tablespoon minced cilantro
½ cup roasted peanuts

SPICE, CRACKLE, AND POP

MAKES *about 8 cups*

PREP/COOK TIME: *5 minutes*

¼ cup vegetable oil

**Pinch of asafetida
(optional)**

**2 teaspoons black mustard
seeds**

**1 teaspoon ground
turmeric**

**¾ cup roasted, salted
peanuts**

**½ cup roasted, salted
cashews**

**6 cups puffed rice cereal
such as Rice Krispies**

**1 cup thin sev such as
Deep brand (optional;
see Note)**

¾ cup golden raisins

1 tablespoon sugar

**¼ teaspoon ground
coriander**

¼ teaspoon ground cumin

1 teaspoon fennel seeds

**¼ teaspoon dried mango
powder**

This sweet/salty/tangy/crunchy mix takes only a few minutes to make, but please have all the ingredients ready before you start cooking, as they are added in quick succession. While traditional recipes for this mix use beaten rice flakes, this one uses Rice Krispies.

Watch the heat carefully, as the cereal can burn easily. Once you have mastered this basic recipe, you can make it your own; try adding dried mango, dried apple, or dried cranberries for color and zing. I love to add red chile flakes just before serving.

Serve this recipe with drinks, as an after-school snack—or be like my son who often asks, "Can I have the Indian Rice Krispies for breakfast, please?" This mix will keep in an airtight container for up to a week.

. . . .

1. Heat the oil in a 5- to 6-quart nonstick saucepan over medium-high heat. When hot, add the asafetida and mustard seeds and stir until the seeds begin to pop, about 30 seconds.

2. Reduce the heat to low and add the turmeric, peanuts, and cashews. Stir for about 30 seconds, until the nuts are completely covered with the flavored oil.

3. Keeping the heat on the lowest possible setting, add the cereal and stir until it is completely covered with spiced oil and golden throughout, about 1 minute.

4. Remove from the heat. Add the sev (if using), raisins, sugar, coriander, cumin, fennel seeds, and mango powder. Continue to mix—your hands are your best tools here—until the cereal is well coated with the spices, about 2 minutes.

5. Let the mix cool completely. Serve immediately or store in an airtight container.

Note: This recipe uses sev (gram flour vermicelli), a very versatile ingredient. When I was growing up, a distant aunt showed me how to make it—it is a long, tedious, and involved process and we are lucky that we can now buy it ready-made at the Indian grocery stores! You can sprinkle it on salads, top plain yogurt with it, or even just munch on it as is.

Shrimp à la José with Coconut Dipping Sauce

Makes *6 appetizer servings*
(*¼ cup sauce per person*)
Prep/Cook time:
20 minutes

1 small red onion, minced
2 small tomatoes, pureed
One 13.5-ounce can
  unsweetened coconut
  milk
1 teaspoon cumin seeds
1 teaspoon red chile
  powder
1-inch piece fresh ginger,
  peeled and minced
1 tablespoon
  Worcestershire sauce
Table salt
24 cooked large shrimp,
  shelled but with tail on

This recipe is what happens when people hang around Chef José Andrés (owner of the Washington, D.C., restaurants Zaytinya, Oyamel, and Jaleo, among others) for too long! I got to know Chef José after interviewing him for several articles and dining at his lovely restaurants over the years; we developed a friendship based on mutual respect and love of cooking. I love, love, love the way José plays with ingredients. He is never afraid to try new flavor combinations and is willing to take risks that may not all be successful. In fact, his focus always seems to be on what can go right and oh, how right things go with his recipes! One thing that has particularly fascinated me is his ability to take a simple recipe and make it elegant: serving eggs and toast with caviar or wrapping anchovies around peaches for an appetizer.

A few months ago, I watched him tape his PBS series, *Made in Spain*, and came away very inspired. I was determined to learn this "play with your ingredients" skill. His words of advice to me were timeless: "Just respect the ingredients and your heritage and you will not go wrong." I kept that advice at the forefront as I attempted to deconstruct one of my favorite curries to serve as an appetizer. I love the deep flavors of this dish and always wanted to do something inspired with it. So here, with all due credit and respect to José Andrés, is my deconstructed version of a creamy shrimp curry.

. . . .

1. Combine the onion, tomatoes, coconut milk, cumin, chile powder, ginger, and Worcestershire sauce in a large bowl and mix well. Taste to check the seasoning. Add salt if needed.

2. Pour the mixture into a deep saucepan and bring to a boil over medium heat.

3. Reduce the heat and simmer for about 20 minutes, until the flavors are melded and the coconut milk has begun to thicken. This sauce has a tendency to splatter, so use a splatter guard.

4. Remove from the heat and allow to come to room temperature.

5. Process in a blender until smooth. This is served at room temperature but you can warm it a bit if you like; I leave it to your taste

6. Divide the mixture among six small martini glasses and place four shrimp on the rim of each glass, or serve it in a bowl as a dipping sauce with the shrimp on the side. Serve immediately.

Beet Salad
with Yogurt Dressing

Serves 4

Prep/Cook time:
10 minutes hands-on, plus 50
minutes for baking the beets

For the Beets:

4 medium beets, different
colors if possible,
trimmed

½ teaspoon ground white
pepper

2 tablespoons vegetable
oil

1 teaspoon table salt

1 tablespoon ground
coriander (see Note)

For the Dressing:

¾ cup plain yogurt,
stirred (see page 21)

¼ teaspoon minced peeled
fresh ginger

½ teaspoon sugar

⅛ teaspoon table salt

In traditional Indian cooking beets are either steamed or boiled. I prefer to roast them in the oven. I find that this releases their true flavor. If you can find different colored beets, it makes for a prettier salad, but red beets taste just fine.

A note about the dressing: When you begin to drizzle it on the beets, the first thought you will have is that it is a lot of dressing! Drizzle a bit, wait a few minutes, and then drizzle some more. The beets will absorb the dressing. Also, there is about a tablespoon of extra dressing since I find many people ask for more of this dressing once they begin eating the salad!

. . . .

To roast the beets

1. Preheat the oven to 425°F. Wash the beets well and pat them dry.

2. In a medium bowl, combine the pepper, oil, salt, and coriander. Add the beets and mix well.

3. Place the beets on a large piece of aluminum foil, and wrap tightly ensuring that they stay in a single layer. Make sure the package is tightly closed to keep the steam inside as the beets cook. (If you are using different colors of beets, wrap each color separately.) Discard any remaining marinade. Place the foil packets on a rimmed baking sheet and bake for about 50 minutes, until the beets are cooked through. Beets are cooked through when they are easily pierced with a knife.

4. Remove from the oven and allow to cool to room temperature.

5. Remove the beets from the foil. You will notice that the skin peels off very easily with your fingers or a paring knife. The spice marinade may have concentrated itself on parts of a beet. If so, gently scrape it off.

6. Cut the beets in wedges and arrange on a plate.

TO MAKE THE DRESSING:

7. Place all the dressing ingredients in a bowl and whisk to combine. If you prefer a thinner dressing, you can add a little water but do not add any oil to this dressing.

8. Place the beets on a serving platter and spoon on the dressing. Serve immediately.

Note: Take my word for it, if you want to increase the flavor of any dish which calls for ground coriander, grind it fresh. It will take you under three minutes to do so and it will add 200 times the flavor of store-bought ground coriander. In my cooking classes, this is one ingredient that I grind in front of my students to show them the difference, and they always, without exception, gasp when the smell the lemony fragrance of freshly ground coriander seeds.

(continued on next page)

How to grind spices: There are a few simple rules to follow when grinding spices.

1. Always be sure you are using fresh, whole spices. Use your nose to tell!

2. You can either grind the spices with a mortar and pestle (using some elbow grease) or a spice grinder. No matter which one you choose, make sure it is dry and clean before you use it.

3. If you are using a grinder, make sure you keep it solely for spices (i.e., don't grind your coffee beans in it). It will spoil the taste of the coffee and the spices!

Pista-Mirch-Dhaniya (Pistachio-Chile-Coriander) Spread

This spread is wonderful on whole grain crackers. I also love adding it to sandwiches and (confession time) will even eat it straight out of the jar. It keeps for about two days in the fridge; store it in the door of the fridge, where it is less cool. If you refrigerate it, bring it up to room temperature for at least an hour before using, to make spreading easier. Most roasted pistachios are already salted, so you don't need to add any additional salt. Be sure to remove any skins before you use the pistachios.

. . . .

1. Heat a small dry skillet over medium heat. Add the coriander seeds and cook them, stirring frequently, until fragrant. This should take less than 1 minute. Be very vigilant and remove them from the heat as soon as you smell the aroma or they will burn—there is no use for burnt spices!

2. Using a mortar and pestle or a small spice or coffee grinder, grind the seeds to a coarse powder.

3. Combine the coriander, pistachios, paneer, cilantro, oil, and chile powder in a blender and process until you get a smooth paste. You can add a touch more oil to aid with the blending if you need it.

4. Transfer to an airtight container and refrigerate until ready to serve.

MAKES *¼ cup*
PREP/COOK TIME:
5 minutes

1 tablespoon whole coriander seeds
1 cup shelled, skinned roasted pistachios
½ cup cubed paneer
2 to 3 generous tablespoons minced cilantro
¼ cup salad oil or unflavored light oil
½ teaspoon red chile powder or red chile flakes

MAKES *8 crepes*

PREP/COOK TIME:

20 minutes (not including the

Garlic Smashed Potatoes)

FOR THE CREPES:

1 cup chickpea flour

About 1¼ cups water

1 teaspoon red chile
    powder or red chile
    flakes

2 small shallots, diced

1 tablespoon chopped
    cilantro

1 teaspoon carom seeds

1 teaspoon minced peeled
    fresh ginger

¼ teaspoon table salt to
    taste

4 teaspoons vegetable oil

FOR THE FILLING:

2 teaspoons Mint-Cilantro
    Chutney (page 36)

½ cup Garlic Smashed
    Potatoes (page 132)

BABY BESAN CREPES WITH POTATOES

These crepes, a way of life in our house on a Sunday night, are good not only as appetizers but also for light suppers. You can fill them with practically any savory filling that you want. I like filling them with potatoes for a hearty and comforting combination. If you don't have time to prepare the potato filling, you can use plain mashed potatoes or grated paneer seasoned with salt and pepper or just slather on the chutney and enjoy. But the filling can be prepared up to two days ahead and stored in the fridge.

These crepes taste best when served as soon as they are prepared.

. . . .

TO PREPARE THE CREPES:

1. Place the chickpea flour in a bowl and add the water slowly with one hand while mixing it in with the other hand. You can use a spatula but I find using my hands works the best. Keep adding the water and mixing to remove all lumps. The final consistency should be like that of pancake batter, pourable but not thin. Add the chile powder, shallots, cilantro, carom seeds, ginger, and salt and mix well.

2. Heat a small crepe pan or skillet on medium heat. Add ½ teaspoon of vegetable oil. Pour in about ¼ cup of the batter (the crepes should be about ⅓ inch thick). Cook for 2 to 3 minutes, until bubbles begin to form. Using a spatula, lift the crepe and flip it over. If it does not flip easily, it needs to cook about a minute longer. After flipping, cook for another 2 to 3 minutes.

Remove from the pan and place on a plate lined with a paper towel. Continue until all the batter is used, with paper between each layer. These crepes are not soft; they are, in fact, a bit crispy.

TO FILL AND SERVE:

1. Place the crepes on plates.

2. Spread each crepe with ¼ teaspoon of the chutney.

3. Top each crepe with about 1 tablespoon of potatoes. Flatten the mound and fold the crepes in half. Serve immediately.

Note: Chickpea flour, or *besan,* a high carb, no-gluten flour, is sold in Indian grocery stores. It tends to become lumpy when water or other liquid is added, so be sure to take all the lumps out before cooking. It is used in making many curries, vegetables, and desserts.

ROASTED SPICY FIG YOGURT

SERVES 6

PREP/COOK TIME:

20 minutes

6 to 8 ripe figs, any
variety, stems trimmed

1 cup plain Greek-style
yogurt

2 tablespoons sweetened
shredded coconut

½ teaspoon ground
cinnamon

¼ teaspoon ground cloves

2 tablespoons coarsely
chopped walnut pieces

3 tablespoons liquid
honey

Figs, or *anjeer*, are very popular in India, particularly in the north. They are usually used in desserts; here, I serve them as a summer appetizer. Presentation is key. I serve mine in small margarita glasses or decorative glass bowls to show off the figs. This recipe uses very ripe figs. If you cannot find fresh figs, I highly recommend Nutra Figs from California. Just dice them up and toss them on top of the yogurt.

. . . .

1. Preheat the oven to 500°F. Cut an X about ½-inch deep on top of the figs. Pull them very gently to separate the pieces just a little. (Do not pull the figs totally apart.)

2. Place the figs on a baking sheet and roast for 10 to 12 minutes, until tender and caramelized. Remove from the oven and allow to cool until you can handle them.

3. Divide the yogurt equally among six serving bowls, about 2 tablespoons per bowl. Gently place the figs on top of the yogurt and sprinkle with the coconut.

4. Mix the cinnamon and cloves in a small bowl. Sprinkle about ⅛ teaspoon of this spice mix over each serving. Sprinkle a few pieces of walnut around the figs. Drizzle with honey, about ½ tablespoon per serving. Serve immediately.

Did you know . . . the ripest figs are like beggars? I read a saying once that perfectly describes how to pick a ripe fig. "It should have the cloak of a beggar and the eye of a widow." In other words, a ripe fig's skin should be broken—tattered like the cloak of a beggar—and it should have slight cracks bursting with its sweet syrup—like the crying eye of a widow.

If the Egyptians Could Do It...

When ancient Egyptians were prepared for their journey to the Other Side, they were well provided with the necessities of life. Among the things that they might take along were the foods and drinks they enjoyed most in life. If we still practiced this ritual today I hope someone would make sure I had a plentiful supply of chaat masala to enjoy on my journey!

Chaat masala is a magical mix of spices that North Indians, particularly Delhi-ites—*Dilliwalas*—like to sprinkle on their snacks. Typically the mix consists of dried ginger, mango powder, red chiles, black salt, and more. Chaat means "to lick" and masala means "spice mix," so I guess it means lick-able spice mix or a spice mix that makes you lick your fingers! While people do try to make it at home, my opinion is why mess with perfection——MDH and Shan make some of the best packaged chaat masala in the world. These brands provide a perfect mix of the tangy and salty flavor that I so crave.

My first memorable encounter with chaat masala was several years ago at home in Bahrain. My mother used to sprinkle it on all our after-school snacks—it went on top of fresh fruits, pieces of pan-fried paneer, inside chutney sandwiches, on top of various fritters, on top of yogurt . . . you name it, and we sprinkled it on top of that dish! The salty, tangy flavor of the spice mix would bring out the best of almost any dish. I remember a trip to the Far East when I brought a small white paper bag of chaat masala with me. I sprinkled it on noodles, fried rice, and just about any fruit I could lay my hands on. I would even try to open it discreetly in restaurants. Of course, I was fourteen and being discreet was not my best talent. The looks on people's faces as they watched me smuggle out some of the mix, suggested that perhaps I dealt in hashish!

My love affair with chaat masala has endured over the years. During my first pregnancy, I think I must have gone through at least two boxes of the mix. (Compare this to the fact that a box usually lasts me about six months.) Through my second pregnancy, it gained another fan—my seven-year-old son. He and I took some with us on our vacation in North Carolina and proceeded to sprinkle it on steamed crab legs, shrimp, and even onion rings. Yum! We now carry it with us to McDonalds (it's great on fries), to picnics (it's great on watermelon) and I even sneak it into his baseball practices (it is good to just place in the palm of your hand and lick)!

So please be kind—for my final journey, sprinkle a little chaat masala before you bid me adieu over the Ganges! ✳

POMEGRANATE-MANGO TOSS

This is a summer must-have. It is a perfect topping for a grilled chicken breast or as a substitute for salsa, and is even good as a light salad when served on buttery Boston lettuce.

. . . .

Mix all the ingredients in a bowl and cover. Leave aside for about 10 minutes or so to let the flavors meld before serving.

SERVES *4*

PREP TIME: *10 minutes*

1 cup fresh pomegranate
   seeds
1 small green mango,
   peeled and diced
2 tablespoons dry-roasted
   peanuts, coarsely
   ground
½ teaspoon red chile
   powder or red chile
   flakes
1 tablespoon lime juice
½ cup shelled cooked
   edamame
One 11-ounce can
   mandarin oranges,
   drained and diced
1 tablespoon chopped
   fresh cilantro
1 teaspoon sugar

INDIAN ONION RINGS WITH CHAAT MASALA

Serves *4 to 6*

PREP/COOK TIME: *25 minutes*

2 medium red onions, sliced into ¼-inch-thick rounds

1 cup all-purpose or chickpea flour

¼ teaspoon table salt to start

½ teaspoon red chile powder

¼ teaspoon carom seeds

1 tablespoon dried fenugreek leaves

2 cups plus 1 teaspoon vegetable oil

1 cup club soda

2 cups vegetable oil

Store-bought chaat masala, as needed

*S*everal fast food places in India serve these light and crispy rings on a large metal rod that looks like a kitchen paper-towel holder. They are easy to make, fun to eat, and wonderful when it is raining outside! I like to use all-purpose flour here but you can use the traditional chickpea flour if you wish.

. . . .

1. Separate the onions into rings. Set aside the very small rings and hard center part for another purpose.

2. In a large bowl, combine the flour, salt, chile powder, carom seeds, fenugreek, and 1 teaspoon of the vegetable oil. Add the club soda a little bit at a time and mix well to ensure that there are no lumps. The batter should be thicker than a pancake batter. If the batter becomes too thin, you can add an additional table-spoon of flour.

3. Add the onions to the batter and make sure that they are well coated.

4. Heat the 2 cups of oil in a deep saucepan to 350°F. Line a baking sheet with a double layer of paper towels.

5. Add a few onion rings at a time to the hot oil and fry, turning them in the oil until they are golden brown on all sides, 2 to 3 minutes.

6. Using a slotted spoon, remove the rings from the oil and place on the paper towels to drain.

7. Continue until all the rings are done. Please note that the temperature of the oil may fall between batches, so allow time for the oil to reheat.

8. Serve the onion rings dusted with chaat masala. Serve immediately.

Did you know . . . carom seed (*ajwain*) is well known in India for its digestive properties. My dad still gives it to me to chew raw if I have a stomach ache. Practitioners of Ayurveda advise gently heating it in a skillet and inhaling the aroma for helping clear nasal passages.

PAPAD STUFFED
WITH PANEER AND CRAB

MAKES *20 pieces*

PREP/COOK TIME:
15 minutes

For the Paneer Filling:

1 cup diced paneer
(½-inch cubes)

1 teaspoon red chile
powder or red chile
flakes

Table salt

For the Crab Filling:

½ cup lump crabmeat
such as Phillips brand,
picked over (select
about 20 large pieces)

1 teaspoon paprika

¼ teaspoon table salt to
start

For Deep Frying:

2 cups vegetable oil

Ten 4-inch diameter
papads

Water as needed

20 toothpicks

Store-bought chaat
masala for garnish

The credit for this recipe goes solely to my aunt, Kanta. *Papad* (lentil wafers) come in two types primarily: the ones you deep fry and the ones you don't! The ones that are *not* deep fried are cooked over an open flame or in the microwave. This recipe uses the deep-fried papad (try the Lakshmi brand—they taste wonderful and are the perfect bite-size). While the papad do keep crisp for up to an hour, the dish tastes better served immediately, so make them a few moments before your guests arrive. The key to making this dish is learning how long to soak the papad in water: just until the papad begin to crumple, any longer and they will soften too much and tear, and then become impossible to fill.

. . . .

To make the paneer filling:

1. In a bowl combine the paneer and chile powder. Add salt to taste and toss to combine. Set aside.

To make the crab filling:

2. In another bowl, combine the crabmeat, paprika, and salt and toss gently to combine. Set aside in the refrigerator.

To fry the papad:

3. Heat the oil in a deep fryer or a deep saucepan to 350°F. Line a baking sheet with a double layer of paper towels.

4. While the oil is heating, prepare the papad: Soak 2 or 3 pieces of the papad in warm water until they are pliable. It takes about a minute or so. Remove the papad from the water and cut each in half.

5. Fill half of the papad pieces with the crab filling and the other half with the paneer filling. Fold over the edges and make sure they overlap. Secure with a toothpick. Continue until all the papad pieces have been filled.

6. Place them in the oil, a few at a time, as you would paper boats in water—gently, with the toothpick side up.

7. Deep-fry each piece for a few seconds or so, until the outside is totally crisp.

8. Remove using a slotted spoon and set on the paper towels to drain.

9. To serve, place the filled papads on a platter, dust lightly with chaat masala, and serve immediately.

THE INDIAN "BURGER"

SERVES *4*

PREP/COOK TIME:

35 minutes (including time to boil potatoes, if needed)

2 tablespoons vegetable
   oil

1 teaspoon cumin seeds

¼ cup finely chopped red
   onion

½ teaspoon black salt

1 teaspoon sugar

½ teaspoon ground
   turmeric

1 teaspoon dried mango
   powder

½ teaspoon red chile
   powder or red chile
   flakes, or less if you like
   less heat

2 medium Idaho potatoes,
   boiled, peeled, and
   mashed

2 tablespoons dry-roasted
   peanuts

1 tablespoon minced
   cilantro

Burgers are not unique to the Western world. An Indian version, bread stuffed with potatoes, has been sold on the roads of India for centuries now. The Indian burger is loaded with chutneys, spices, and fresh herbs. This particular one is an adaptation of a burger sold on the streets of western India. The key is to use plain bread buns—no sesame seeds or onions on the rolls, please. If you have an Indian grocery nearby, stop in and see if it has the traditional Indian *pau* bread, as it works well for this recipe.

Have all your ingredients set out and ready to go. The spices are added in quick succession, and if you start looking for something in the middle of the recipe, you will burn the spices!

. . . .

1. Heat the vegetable oil in a large skillet over medium heat until it shimmers.

2. Add the cumin seeds. As soon as they begin to sizzle add the onion. Cook for 1 to 2 minutes, until the onion just begins to change color.

3. Add the black salt, sugar, turmeric, mango powder, chile powder, and potatoes. Mix well.

4. Continue to cook for 1 to 2 minutes, until the mixture has completely heated through.

5. Remove from the heat and allow the mixture to come to room temperature.

6. When you are ready to serve, reheat the potato mixture. It should be warmed through but not hot.

7. Add the peanuts and cilantro to the potato mixture. Mix well and divide the mixture into four equal portions. Flatten them as you would hamburger patties. These are very delicate patties, so be gentle. Set the patties aside.

8. Heat a large skillet or griddle over medium heat. Butter the inside of your buns. Place the buns buttered side down in the skillet and toast until golden. Remove from the heat.

9. Spread about 1 teaspoon of the tamarind-date chutney on one side of a bun and 1 teaspoon of the mint-cilantro chutney on the other side. Place the patty on top of one of the bun halves, sprinkle some sev on top, and close with the other side of the bun. Serve immediately.

2 tablespoons unsalted butter

4 hamburger buns or *pau* bread

4 teaspoons store-bought tamarind-date chutney (page 35)

4 teaspoons Mint-Cilantro Chutney (page 36)

1 tablespoon sev (page 20)

CURRIED CARROT AND GINGER SOUP WITH PAN-FRIED PANEER

SERVES 6

PREP/COOK TIME:

50 minutes, mostly unattended

3 tablespoons vegetable
oil

1 cup paneer, cut into
½-inch cubes

Table salt

2 tablespoons unsalted
butter

2 medium leeks, white
and pale green parts
only, peeled and
coarsely chopped

1 pound carrots, peeled
and sliced

1 red or orange bell
pepper, seeded and
diced

1 tablespoon minced
peeled fresh ginger

½ teaspoon ground
turmeric

use paneer instead of bread as croutons here. If you don't have paneer, you can substitute firm tofu. This soup tastes better if it is allowed to sit for a day in the fridge; it helps all the flavors meld. I add just a touch of red chile powder or red chile flakes here; if you like more heat, go ahead and add more. One more thing—use full-grown carrots, please. The baby carrots are great for dipping and munching but they are lacking in sweetness and depth of flavor. Watch the salt carefully as prepared stock is generally already salted.

. . . .

1. Heat the oil in a wok or large nonstick skillet over medium-high heat. Add the paneer and fry for 6 to 8 minutes, until lightly browned. Remove immediately—do not overcook, as this will make the paneer rubbery. Just a slight golden brown color indicates that the paneer is cooked. Remove paneer with a slotted spoon and drain on paper towels. Sprinkle with salt to taste.

2. Melt the butter in a medium (3-quart) lidded saucepan over medium heat. Add the leeks and cook for 6 to 7 minutes, until translucent.

3. Add the carrots, bell pepper, and ginger and cook for another 5 to 7 minutes, until the carrots begin to soften.

4. Add the turmeric, chile powder, and coriander and mix well. Cook for another minute.

5. Add the stock and bring to a boil. Reduce the heat, cover, and simmer for about 20 minutes or until the vegetables are very tender.

6. Remove from heat and allow to cool to room temperature.

7. Working in batches, puree the soup in a blender.

8. Stir in the cream. Add salt and pepper to taste.

9. Reheat before serving. Serve warm, topped with the paneer and sprigs of cilantro.

⅛ teaspoon red chile powder or red chile flakes

1 tablespoon ground coriander

5 cups vegetable stock or chicken stock

1 cup light cream

Freshly ground black pepper

Fresh cilantro sprigs for garnish

LYCHEE-PINEAPPLE SALAD

SERVES *4*

PREP/COOK TIME:

15 minutes

1 cup diced seeded lychees

1 cup diced blood or navel
oranges (peeled)

½ cup diced cucumber (1
small peeled mini-
cucumber such as the
Wee Babee brand)

½ cup diced pineapple
(about ¼ small)

1 cup diced mango (about
1 medium)

½ cup diced pear (1 small
Bosc, cored)

2 tablespoons fresh lime
juice (1 small lime)

½ teaspoon red chile
flakes (optional)

1 tablespoon minced
cilantro

Freshly ground pepper

¼ teaspoon store-bought
chaat masala (see page
16)

Make this salad when you feel like something sweet for
lunch. It takes a few minutes to pull together but is very
filling and satisfying for the sweet tooth without being unhealthy.
The chaat masala used here adds the savory flavor so you don't
need to add any additional salt.

. . . .

Place the lychees, oranges, cucumber, pineapple, mango, pear,
lime juice, chile flakes (if using), and cilantro in a large bowl and
toss gently to combine. Add pepper to taste. Just before serving,
sprinkle with the chaat masala.

Paneer Cups

These are like crustless mini quiches. They are fairly mild and the kids love them. When I serve them to adult friends, I always add a dot of my favorite spicy chutney on top.

. . . .

1. Preheat oven to 350°F. Spray a regular 12-cup muffin pan with nonstick cooking spray. Do this liberally as the paneer cups have a tendency to stick if the surface is not well greased.

2. Heat the butter in a medium skillet over medium-high heat. Add the pepper, mushrooms, cilantro, and green chiles. Cook for about 5 minutes, stirring frequently, until the peppers are soft.

3. Add the curry powder and mix well. Cook for another minute. Remove from the heat and allow to cool to room temperature.

4. In a medium bowl, whisk together the eggs, cream, paneer, cheddar cheese, baking mix, salt, and pepper. (Watch the salt here, as the vegetables are cooked in salted butter already.)

5. Add the vegetables to the egg and cheese mixture and mix well.

6. Divide the mixture among the muffin cups, about ¼ cup each.

7. Bake until the eggs are just set and a knife inserted in the center comes out clean, 30 to 35 minutes.

8. Allow to cool for 5 minutes in the muffin pan, then run a knife around sides of each cup to release. Serve immediately.

MAKES *12 large pieces (1 per person)*
PREP/COOK TIME: *50 minutes, including 35 minutes to bake*

Nonstick cooking spray
2 tablespoons salted butter
1 cup finely chopped red bell pepper (about 1 medium)
1 cup cleaned and finely chopped mushrooms
2 tablespoons finely minced cilantro
2 small green serrano chiles, minced
1 teaspoon hot Madras curry powder
4 large eggs
1 cup heavy cream
1 cup finely grated paneer
1 cup grated mild cheddar cheese
½ cup baking mix such as Bisquick
¼ teaspoon table salt to start
¼ teaspoon freshly ground black pepper to start

SAVORY MINI CHEESECAKES WITH RED PEPPER AND GREEN TOMATILLO CHUTNEY

MAKES *30 pieces*

PREP/COOK TIME:
25 minutes

Nonstick cooking spray
30 mini phyllo shells such
    as the Organic Mini
    Fillo Shells from the
    Fillo Factory
One 8-ounce package
    cream cheese, softened
1 medium egg
5 tablespoons sour cream
3 tablespoons Red Pepper
    and Green Tomatillo
    Chutney (page 38)

Plain savory cheesecakes provide a great base for showing off spicy chutneys. I use my Red Pepper and Green Tomatillo Chutney but you can use any one for this dish. This is always a smash hit at parties and super easy to make.

. . . .

1. Preheat the oven to 350°F. Grease a baking sheet with nonstick cooking spray. Arrange the phyllo shells on the sheet.

2. Whisk together the cheese, egg, and sour cream until well combined.

3. Place 2 teaspoons of the mixture into each shell. Bake for 15 minutes or until the filling is firm and set.

4. Remove from the oven and cool to room temperature.

5. Top each cheesecake with about ¼ teaspoon of the chutney and serve.

VEGETABLES, BEANS, and LENTILS

．．．．．．．．．．．．．．．．．．．．．．．．．．．．．．．．

ndia serves a mind-boggling variety of vegetables, many of which have still not reached America.

These recipes use Indian techniques and Indian spices but I have to confess to sneaking in vegetables like Brussels sprouts and leeks from my adopted home. They are intentionally short on ingredients; the number of ingredients doesn't matter. What matters is that you are using the right spice to lend the correct flavor to the vegetables. Spice should complement the vegetables and not overwhelm them.

Needless to say, use fresh vegetables where you can find them. It adds tremendously to the flavor of the dish. If you can't find fresh, then use frozen vegetables. I am not fond of canned vegetables.

Visit your local Indian grocer and check out the vegetables in both the fresh and the frozen sections. I can guarantee you that you will be pleasantly surprised to find some familiar vegetables like okra, and some unfamiliar ones, like lotus root. Buy them, and try them; you have nothing to lose and a lot of new tastes to gain.

One thing I have learned from my visits to my local Indian store is to approach friendly looking shoppers in the store and ask them what to do with unfamiliar vegetables. Almost always, the people I approach are helpful. (Yes, even I don't know all about every vegetable the Indian grocery store sells. There are so many different communities of Indians eating so many different types of vegetables that I find myself, gladly, in the role of a perpetual student.)

Pan-Fried Zucchini and Yellow Squash with Cumin

This has got to be one of my favorite Monday night recipes, because it's so simple and quick. You can vary the taste by changing the spice from cumin to coriander or mustard seeds. I don't peel the zucchini but you can if you prefer.

. . . .

1. Heat the oil in a large skillet over medium heat. Add the cumin seeds. When the seeds begin to sizzle, add the zucchini, squash, and bell pepper.

2. Fry the vegetables over high heat until they soften and begin to brown, 8 to 9 minutes.

3. Add the turmeric and chile flakes and cook for another minute, until the spices are well mixed with the vegetables. Stir in salt to taste.

4. Serve hot, sprinkled with lemon juice and garnished with cilantro.

Did you know . . . Wolfgang Puck told me, "Peppers are one of those vegetables most often found to be heavy in pesticides and other chemical residues. So, I strongly recommend you purchase them from your organic greengrocer or on a visit to your farmers' market."

SERVES *4*

PREP/COOK TIME:
15 minutes

2 tablespoons vegetable oil

1½ teaspoons cumin seeds

1 large zucchini, diced

1 small yellow squash, diced

½ organic red bell pepper, seeded and diced (see Note)

½ teaspoon ground turmeric

½ teaspoon red chile flakes

Table salt

½ tablespoon fresh lemon juice

Fresh cilantro leaves for garnish

ACORN SQUASH WITH FIVE SPICES

SERVES 4

PREP/COOK TIME:

35 minutes, mostly unattended

¼ cup vegetable oil

½ teaspoon cumin seeds

1½ teaspoons store-
   bought paanch phoron

Pinch of asafetida

2 large or 4 to 6 small
   organic shallots, diced

1 small green serrano
   chile, minced

1 dried whole red chile

3½ cups (about 1
   medium) acorn
   squash, seeded, peeled,
   and diced (¼-inch
   dice)

¼ teaspoon table salt to
   start

½ teaspoon ground
   turmeric

½ cup water

Warm honey (optional)

The mixture of five spices called *paanch phoron*—equal parts whole cumin, fennel, fenugreek, onion seeds, and mustard seeds—is common in eastern India, and adds potent flavors to the squash. Honestly, once you start using this spice mix, you will wonder why you never did before, as the spices work so harmoniously together. You can buy the premixed spices at most Indian grocers. I like to drizzle a little honey just before I serve this dish as I feel it brings out all the spicy flavors. Be sure the honey is warm and use just about two teaspoons.

I use acorn squash since our family loves the taste but it can be a bit hard to peel. Choose a squash whose ridges are not too deep. I usually cut it into wedges along the grooves, and then peel off the skin. You can use a winter squash of your choice, just be sure to adjust the cooking time. Cook until squash is tender.

. . . .

1. Heat the oil in a deep lidded saucepan over medium heat. When the oil begins to shimmer, add the cumin seeds, paanch phoron, asafetida, and shallots. Cook for about 2 minutes, until the shallots begin to change color.

2. Add the green chile, red chile, and the squash and mix well. Add the salt and turmeric and mix. Raise the heat and cook over medium-high heat for about 5 minutes, until the squash just begins to brown.

3. Add water and bring to a boil. Cover and cook over low heat until the squash is totally soft and the water has almost dried up, about 20 minutes.

4. Serve hot (drizzled with warm honey if desired).

CARAMELIZED SHALLOTS
AND TURNIPS WITH ONION SEEDS

Turnips are such undervalued vegetables. I love their mild taste. They never misbehave when I cook them and always reward me with delight in each bite.

This dish is a deep yellow if served immediately but will change to an attractive dark brown if refrigerated to serve later.

. . . .

1. In a deep lidded saucepan, heat the oil over medium heat. When the oil shimmers add the onion seeds, shallots, and turnips and cook for 5 to 6 minutes, until the vegetables begin to brown.

2. Add the turmeric, red chile powder, salt, and sugar and mix well. Cook for another minute.

3. Add the water, cover, and cook over low heat for 15–20 minutes, until the turnips are soft. Serve hot.

SERVES *4*

PREP/COOK TIME:
30 minutes

2 tablespoons vegetable
   oil
1 teaspoon onion seeds
4 large or 10 to 12 small
   organic shallots,
   quartered
5 small turnips, peeled
   and cut in ¼-inch dice
   (about 2¾ cups)
1 teaspoon ground
   turmeric
1 teaspoon red chile
   powder or red chile
   flakes
¼ teaspoon table salt to
   start
½ teaspoon sugar
¼ cup water

"GOURDED SECRETS"

SERVES *4*

PREP/COOK TIME:
Marinating time is about an hour and cooking time is 30 minutes.

5 or 6 small (5-inch) bitter gourds (see Note)

Table salt

2 tablespoons vegetable oil

1 small red onion, chopped

1 teaspoon grated peeled fresh ginger

1 teaspoon coriander seeds, roughly pounded

1 teaspoon red chile powder or red chile flakes

½ teaspoon dried mango powder

Chopped fresh cilantro for garnish

*K*arela, the ridged Indian gourd, has a very bitter taste. My mother taught me to marinate it in salt for a few hours to get the bitterness out. Several friends and aunts swear that sprinkling salt and turmeric on it and leaving it overnight has the same effect. In either case, the gourd should be rinsed before proceeding with the recipe. If you have never tried bitter gourds, this will add a new vegetable to your repertoire and is perfect for a lovely spring dinner.

. . . .

1. Scrape the ridged part of the gourds with a knife or a vegetable peeler. They are a bit messy to peel so I do it over a sink. Cut into ¼-inch-thick rounds. Place the rounds in a bowl and salt them liberally. Leave for 30 minutes to an hour.

2. Rinse the gourds well to remove all the salt. Pat dry.

3. In a large lidded skillet, heat the oil over medium heat. When the oil begins to shimmer, add the onion, ginger, and the gourd slices. Cook for 8 to 10 minutes, until the gourd is crisp and the onions have changed color to a light brown.

4. Add the coriander seeds, chile powder, and mango powder, and salt to taste and mix well.

5. Add about ¼ cup water, cover, and cook over low heat until the gourd is soft and all the water dries up, 5 to 7 minutes.

6. Remove from the heat, garnish with cilantro, and serve hot.

To pound coriander seeds: Use a mortar and pestle to pound the seeds enough to break them up or add to a heavy-duty plastic bag and pound with a rolling pin to break the seeds into pieces.

Note: When you cut the gourd, inspect the seeds. If they are white then you are fine, but if the seeds are red then the gourd is too bitter and will not lose its bitterness even by salting. Discard it!

GRIDDLED VEGETABLES

SERVES 6

PREP/COOK TIME:

40 minutes

1 teaspoon coriander
seeds

1 teaspoon cumin seeds

1 teaspoon dried
pomegranate seeds
(optional)

1 tablespoon dried
fenugreek leaves

2 or 3 whole cloves

1 whole green cardamom
pod

1 teaspoon black mustard
seeds

1 teaspoon dried mango
powder

A pinch of black salt or ¼
teaspoon table salt

1 medium Idaho potato,
peeled and sliced
lengthwise about ¼-
inch thick

This is one of the simplest yet most flavorful ways to cook vegetables. They are coated in a dry spice rub and then cooked on a griddle. Cooking on a hot griddle, or *tava* cooking used to be very popular in India years ago and is making a comeback with Indian Americans. A real time saver here——MDH brand sells a wonderful packaged spice mix called "Tava Fry Masala" that you can use in this recipe instead of the rub indicated here. Don't use frozen or canned vegetables for this——fresh only, please.

To save on cooking time, I will sometimes use a skillet instead of a griddle and cover the vegetables to generate steam.

. . . .

1. Grind together the coriander, cumin, pomegranate seeds (if using), fenugreek, cloves, cardamon, mustard, mango powder, and salt in a spice grinder or coffee grinder.

2. Lay out the vegetable slices on one or more baking sheets. Cover one side of all the vegetables with the spice rub—you can either just sprinkle the rub over the vegetables or better, use your fingers and gently press some of the rub on the surface of the vegetables.

3. Heat the vegetable oil on a flat griddle on medium heat. When the oil shimmers, add the vegetables, spice side up, in a single layer. To reduce cooking time, add similar vegetables at the same time. All the vegetables will take about the same time to cook; if you have a griddle large enough, add them all together. Otherwise cook them in batches and keep warm on a baking sheet in a low oven.

4. As the bottoms of the vegetables begin to brown, sprinkle a few drops of water on the vegetables; this will generate some steam and help the vegetables to cook faster.

5. When the bottom starts to brown, flip once, reduce the heat to low and continue to cook until the vegetables are cooked through.

6. Serve immediately.

$\mathcal{D}$id you know . . . According to the Patak's website, "One teaspoon of *amchur* (dried mango powder) has the equivalent acidity of three tablespoons of lemon juice." Patak's is a leading manufacturer of Indian spices and pickles. Its hot lime pickle and eggplant pickle (called an aubergine pickle) in particular are excellent. Its products are available in many supermarkets.

10 to 12 okra pods, tops cut off and halved lengthwise

1 Italian eggplant (about 4 inches long), top cut off, sliced lengthwise about ¼-inch thick

½ large red onion, sliced horizontally about ¼-inch thick

¼ cup vegetable oil (you may need a little more)

PAN-SEARED EGGPLANT WITH GINGER AND HONEY

SERVES *4*

PREP/COOK TIME:
40 minutes

6 tablespoons vegetable
    oil (more if needed)
1 medium eggplant,
    sliced into ¾-inch-
    thick rounds
Table salt
3 tablespoons Ginger and
    Honey Marinade (page
    42), warmed

Eggplants have been an Indian favorite for centuries. Traditionally, the vegetable is cooked in curries, roasted in the oven and pureed, or even used in *raitas* (yogurt-based side dishes). In this unusual preparation, it is pan-fried and then drizzled with a warm honey sauce. You can also roast the eggplant slices in the oven and then drizzle the marinade. Be flexible with the amount of marinade. I use a little but my husband likes to use several tablespoons. It is not a question of "how much" but of how much you enjoy.

. . . .

1. Heat the oil in a large lidded skillet over medium-low heat. When the oil begins to shimmer, add the eggplant and cook, covered, 12 to 14 minutes on each side, until soft and well browned. If all the eggplant slices don't fit into the skillet, do this using two skillets simultaneously. This way, the first batch won't get cold while you are making the second batch.

2. Remove from the pan and drain on paper towels. Season with salt.

3. Place on a serving platter and drizzle with the marinade. Serve immediately.

Alternatively, you can also roast the eggplant. Preheat the oven to 425°F. Spray a foil-lined baking sheet with nonstick cooking oil. Place the eggplant slices in a single layer on the sheet. Spray the slices with cooking spray and sprinkle with salt. Roast for about 25 minutes, until soft and browned.

Eggplant and Tomatoes with Cilantro

This is our favorite comfort food. The best advice I can give you on this dish is to leave it alone as it cooks. Don't mess with it, don't monkey with it, just leave it and the dish will reward you with dynamic flavors.

I like to slather this onto some crusty bread for a quick, hearty lunch.

. . . .

1. In a deep lidded saucepan, heat the oil over high heat. Add the ginger-garlic paste and stir for about 10 seconds.

2. Add the red chile. Reduce the heat to medium-high. Add the tomatoes, potatoes, and eggplant and cook for 12 to 14 minutes, until the potatoes begin to change color and the tomatoes and eggplant begin to soften.

3. Add the turmeric, red chile powder, and salt, and cook for another minute, stirring to mix well.

4. Add ¼ cup water, bring to a boil, and cover. Lower heat to the lowest setting on your stove and cook for 35 to 40 minutes, until the vegetables have completely cooked through. If the mixture seems dry, you can add another ¼ cup of water and continue to cook until the vegetables are done.

5. Serve hot, garnished with cilantro.

SERVES *4 to 6*

PREP/COOK TIME: *40 minutes, mostly unattended*

3 tablespoons vegetable oil

2 teaspoons store-bought ginger-garlic paste

1 dried red chile, roughly pounded

2 small tomatoes, finely chopped

2 medium Idaho potatoes, peeled and diced

1 medium eggplant (about 1¼ to 1½ pounds), washed and diced

½ teaspoon ground turmeric

1 teaspoon red chile powder (or to taste)

¼ teaspoon table salt

¼ to ½ cup water

2 tablespoons minced cilantro

Garlic Smashed Potatoes

Serves *4*

Prep/Cook time:

*10 minutes (add 15 minutes if
you need to boil the potatoes)*

2 medium Idaho potatoes,
  scrubbed, boiled,
  peeled, and mashed
2 tablespoons unsalted
  butter, melted
Table salt
1 tablespoon vegetable oil
1 teaspoon black mustard
  seeds
2 garlic cloves, minced
2 large or 4 to 6 small
  organic shallots, very
  finely chopped
1 small green serrano
  chile, minced
2 tablespoons
  unsweetened
  desiccated coconut
1 teaspoon red chile
  powder or red chile
  flakes
Fresh cilantro for garnish

This is an adapted version of a recipe that my mother makes. She does not add coconut to her cooking at all. But I do—it is the influence of being married to a man from the western parts of India, where it is rare for them not to add coconut to everything!

You can serve this as a side on its own, as a topping for toasted pita, or in the Baby Besan Crepes with Potatoes (page 104).

. . . .

1. In a bowl combine the potatoes, the melted butter, and salt to taste. Mix well. Set aside.

2. In a medium skillet, heat the vegetable oil on medium heat. When the oil begins to shimmer, add the mustard seeds. When the seeds begin to sizzle, add the garlic, shallots, and the green chile. Cook until the shallots begin to brown, 2 to 3 minutes. Add the coconut and remove from the heat.

3. Add the red chile powder and mix well. Pour this mixture over the potatoes. You can either serve it like this or mix the spices into the potatoes.

4. Garnish with cilantro.

Rice and Black-Eyed Peas with Fresh Crushed Garlic

My dear friend Janet always serves her famous Hoppin' John on New Year's Day. I love the mix of peas and rice. Here is my own rendition; makes for a full and hearty meal.

Fire-roasted tomatoes add a lovely sour note to this dish. If you don't have them, you can use fresh tomatoes. Play with the tastes here—try crushed tomatoes with roasted garlic or leave out the tomatoes and add chopped red onions or sweet Vidalia onions, or change the beans to red kidney beans . . . you get the idea!

* * * * * * * * * * * * * * *

1. In a deep saucepan, heat the vegetable oil. When the oil begins to shimmer, add the garlic and cumin and cook for about 30 seconds.

2. Add the tomatoes and cook over medium-high heat for 8 minutes or until the oil begins to separate from the sides of the tomato. You can use a potato masher to mash down the tomatoes and help them cook faster. If the tomatoes appear to be sticking to the pan, add a little water and continue cooking.

3. Add the turmeric, red chile powder, coriander, and salt. Mix well. Add the black-eyed peas and mix well. Cook for another 2 minutes.

4. Add the rice and water and bring to a boil. Reduce the heat. Cover and simmer over low heat for 10 to 12 minutes, until the water has been completely absorbed.

5. Serve hot, garnished with the scallions and cilantro.

SERVES 6

PREP/COOK TIME: *30 minutes, mostly unattended*

2 tablespoons vegetable oil
2 garlic cloves, crushed
1 teaspoon cumin seeds
One 14.5-ounce can fire-roasted crushed tomatoes such as Muir Glen
½ teaspoon ground turmeric
1 teaspoon red chile powder
2 teaspoons ground coriander
¼ teaspoon table salt, to taste
One 15-ounce can black-eyed peas, drained and rinsed
1 cup basmati rice
2 cups water
2 sliced scallions, white and pale green parts only, for garnish
Fresh cilantro sprigs for garnish

BUTTERNUT SQUASH STEW WITH JAGGERY

MAKES *6 cups, about 6 servings*

PREP/COOK TIME: *About an hour, mostly unattended*

3 tablespoons unsalted butter

1 teaspoon vegetable oil

1 large red onion, sliced

2 or 3 garlic cloves, minced

1-inch piece ginger, peeled and grated

1 tablespoon store-bought sambar powder

1 teaspoon red chile powder or red chile flakes

½ teaspoon tamarind paste

1 medium butternut squash, peeled, seeded, and cut into small chunks

1 small organic red bell pepper, peeled, seeded, and diced (see Note, page 123)

I have always been a huge fan of soups and stews. This one, loaded with vegetables, lentils, and warm spices is perfect for winter! If you don't have sambar powder, you can use curry powder instead. Sambar powder gives this dish a very tangy taste. If you use standard curry powder, the taste will be different, not better or worse, but just different.

If you don't have jaggery on hand, you can use dark brown sugar, but I would strongly suggest that you use this recipe to experiment with jaggery. It has such a unique taste. You can add it to preserves, jams, compotes, cakes (grate it finely), lemonade, lentils, stews, and so much more. In India it is even served raw; there's nothing like a small lump of jaggery to put a smile on one's face.

When I make this dish during my cooking class I'm always asked, why the use of butter and oil, why not just one? Adding a touch of oil prevents the butter from burning (and becoming that ghastly brown color) during the heating process.

. . . .

1. In a 6-quart stockpot or Dutch oven, heat the butter and oil over medium heat.

2. Add the onion, garlic, and ginger and cook 6 to 8 minutes, stirring frequently, until golden and softened.

3. Add the sambar powder and red chile powder and cook for another minute or so.

4. Add the tamarind paste, squash, and bell peppers and cook for another 2 to 3 minutes. Add the salt and sugar and mix well. Add the lentils, broth, and water. Bring to a boil. Reduce the heat to medium-low; cover and simmer until the vegetables and lentils are very tender, about 50 minutes. Serve, garnished with cilantro.

You can also puree this in batches and serve as a hearty soup. If you are going to puree it for the soup, be sure to cool the stew to room temperature before blending it, then reheat to serve.

Note: Caramel-colored jaggery is made from sugarcane juice; there is a darker version available that is called palm jaggery, and you can use that here as well. It is sold in large blocks in the Indian store. I use a hammer to gently break it down into small pieces. Once you break the block, you can also grate the small pieces. While I do substitute brown sugar for jaggery once in a while, please know that they taste different—jaggery has a taste almost like molasses.

1 small organic green bell pepper, peeled, seeded, and diced
¼ teaspoon table salt
½ tablespoon jaggery, palm sugar, or dark brown sugar (see Note)
1 cup red lentils, washed
2 cups low-salt chicken or vegetable broth
2 cups water
Fresh cilantro sprigs for garnish

GREEN BEANS SUBZI

SERVES *4*

PREP/COOK TIME:

25 minutes

2 tablespoons vegetable
  oil
1 teaspoon cumin seeds
2 garlic cloves, crushed
1 small tomato, diced
1 pound baby potatoes,
  peeled and quartered
½ teaspoon ground
  turmeric
½ teaspoon red chile
  powder
1½ teaspoons ground
  coriander
Half of a 16-ounce bag
  frozen cut green beans,
  thawed, or ½ pound
  cut fresh green beans
Table salt
Water, as needed

*F*rozen green beans are God's gift to busy mothers! They cook up in a few minutes, are good for you, and taste great. How can you go wrong with these? This recipe is very versatile. You can use fresh green or yellow beans—just adjust the cooking time.

. . . .

1. In a large lidded skillet, heat the vegetable oil over high heat. When the oil begins to shimmer, add the cumin seeds. When the cumin seeds begin to sizzle, add the garlic, tomato, and potatoes.

2. Cook for 6 to 8 minutes, until the tomato begins to soften.

3. Add the tumeric, red chile powder, coriander, and green beans. Mix well. Add salt to taste. Add about 2 tablespoons water. Cover and cook over low heat for 12 to 15 minutes, until the potatoes are soft and the beans have cooked through.

4. Serve immediately.

ROASTED CAULIFLOWER WITH FENNEL

I owe eGullet.org a lot—it taught me how to cook well and how to take chances with ingredients and cooking methods. This dish is a perfect example. I had made cauliflower every which way——I blanched it, sautéed it, boiled it, mashed it, deep-fried it, and have even eaten it raw. But until eGullet, I never knew I could roast it! This recipe really brings out the richness of the cauliflower and is matched perfectly with the robustness of the spices. I use my fennel rub along with a few other spices. If you have sea salt, it works really well with this recipe. The cauliflower tends to shrink when roasted so one head of cauliflower is about right for 2 servings.

. . . .

1. Preheat the oven to 400°F. Cut the cauliflower into 1-inch florets and place in a large bowl. Drizzle with the oil and toss with your hands to coat each floret.

2. In a small bowl combine the dry rub, coriander, and salt. Add the spice mixture to the cauliflower. Once again, no tool is better than your hands. Get in there and make sure all the florets are well coated.

3. Place the cauliflower on a baking sheet and spread out evenly in a single layer. Don't worry if it is a little crowded. If you really cannot fit it on one sheet, use two.

4. Bake for about 15 minutes. Stir and bake for another 15 minutes or until the cauliflower is well browned and cooked through. Serve hot.

1 medium head cauliflower (about 1¼ to 1½ pounds)

¼ cup vegetable oil

1½ tablespoons Fennel-Chile Dry Rub (page 40)

½ tablespoon coriander seeds, crushed

¼ teaspoon table salt to start

BRUSSELS SPROUTS, LEEKS, AND CURRY LEAVES

SERVES *4*

PREP/COOK TIME:
25 minutes

2 tablespoons vegetable oil

1 teaspoon black mustard seeds

Pinch of asafetida

10 to 15 fresh curry leaves

2 whole dried red chiles, broken

15 Brussels sprouts, trimmed and chopped (about 1 pound)

2 medium leeks, white and green parts only, chopped

3 tablespoons chopped dry-roasted peanuts

½ teaspoon ground turmeric

½ teaspoon red chile powder or red chile flakes

1 teaspoon ground coriander

¼ teaspoon table salt to start

You will never look at Brussels sprouts the same way again after this you try this recipe. While they are not a traditional Indian vegetable, Brussels sprouts have found their way into my kitchen. Honestly, I first tried them to see why so many Americans disliked them! They tasted mostly like mini cabbages but a bit bland so I decided to spice them up a bit. Before using the sprouts, remove a few of the outer leaves if they are hard and damaged. Also, be sure the leeks are clean: after you have chopped them, place them in a bowl of cold water and then strain through a sieve. Place them on a paper towel and pat dry.

. . . .

1. Heat the vegetable oil in a large lidded skillet over medium heat. When the oil shimmers, add the mustard seeds. When the seeds begin to sizzle, add the asafetida, curry leaves, dried chiles, Brussels sprouts, and leeks.

2. Sauté for 5 to 6 minutes on medium heat, until the vegetables begin to brown.

3. Add the peanuts, turmeric, red chile powder, coriander, and salt. Mix well. Cook for another 2 minutes.

4. Add about a tablespoon of water, cover, and reduce the heat to low. Cook for 10 to 12 minutes, until the vegetables are tender and completely cooked through. Serve immediately.

QUICK SPICED PANEER

*H*ere we are using the very traditional eastern Indian spice mix, paanch phoron (see page 17 for more information), a traditional mix of five spices, to spice up a sauté of some Indian cheese. Play with this recipe. Try it first with paneer, and then experiment with vegetables, shrimp, or whatever else suits your fancy.

. . . .

1. Heat the vegetable oil in a medium skillet over medium heat. Add the paanch phoron and asafetida. As soon as the spices sizzle—a few seconds—add the ginger and green chiles. Mix well. Add the shallots and tomato and cook for 2 to 3 minutes, until the shallots begin to change color.

2. Stir in the water and cook until it evaporates, 5 to 7 minutes.

3. Add the paneer and cook for another minute.

4. Add the salt and turmeric and stir to coat well. Cook for 2 to 3 minutes more, until the paneer is heated through. Serve hot.

SERVES 4

PREP/COOK TIME:
15 to 20 minutes

2 tablespoons vegetable oil
2½ teaspoons store-bought paanch phoron (page 17)
Pinch of asafetida
1 teaspoon grated peeled fresh ginger
2 medium green serrano chiles, minced
2 large or 4 to 6 small organic shallots, diced
1 small tomato, diced
¼ cup water
2 cups diced paneer (¼-inch dice)
Table salt to taste
1 teaspoon ground turmeric

What Is Real Cooking?

What is "real cooking"? Who is a "real" cook? I write about food for a living; I should know the answer to these seemingly simple questions, yet I am not entirely sure.

Each time I visit New York I look forward to trying the food in the city's legendary restaurants, but mostly to eating at the home of my friend Vrinda. She is a highly successful investment banker, a bundle of confidence and a complete misfit with traditions. And she is not a cook; not a real one anyway, she repeatedly tells me. You know the ones, she tells me, who can whip up a gourmet dinner for twenty in the blink of an eye; the ones who can prepare rice ninety-seven different ways and then have sixty-five recipes for leftovers.

A few years ago my husband and I visited her at her home near New York City. We arrived in the late morning and were greeted with the warmth of a blossoming friendship. Her apartment overlooked a gorgeous golf course and as her husband began speaking in glowing terms about the view, she retreated to the kitchen to cook lunch. I offered to help. She shrugged her shoulders, "It will be nothing special. Just sit and chat with me as I cook."

I watched her, casually at first and then intently. Meticulous and fast, she was cooking her food in traditional plain stainless-steel utensils that she had brought with her from India. No nonstick pans, no Cuisinart, no high-end chef's knives in this tiny kitchen. She had, however, managed to nail into the counter a mean-looking coconut scraper with a razor-sharp edge.

Her gestures were precise. She has done this before many times, I thought.

Creamy yellow lentils simmered on the right back burner, growling at the spices floating on top of them. Deftly she calmed them by pouring in some oil. The left back burner had a large skillet containing a little oil. She quickly began to sauté thinly sliced onions in it. Then she added a generous helping of cumin seeds and the rice that had been soaking on the side. She sautéed it briefly and then added water that she measured at the sink, one raise of an eyebrow at a time. Impatiently she tapped her fingers on the range. "Come on, *boil*," she commanded. It boiled fast as if to obey. A pinch of salt appeared from nowhere as did a squeeze of lemon juice. She covered it with a lid, reduced the heat, and then turned her attention to the potatoes.

We talked as she diced with mechanical precision. I wonder if she had ever noticed that my potatoes rarely are all the same size. Another pan went on the range. In went a few tablespoons of oil and then mustard seeds. As if in defiance of the heat the seeds began to sputter and rebel. She sprinkled something that I could not see and then added a few whole dried red chiles. The room began to smell divine. Panic set in as she began to look around frantically for something. The garlic! The garlic was needed before the spices began to burn. She found it still crushed under the rolling pin, quickly scooped it up, and added it to the pan. The potatoes went in next; following in quick succession were the ground spices. She talked up a storm as she cooked, not

stopping to measure or taste or analyze. The potatoes were beginning to brown. She turned the heat down, covered the pot and turned to me. "Now," she said, "the salad."

She came to the tiny kitchen table with a large bowl of cucumbers, tomatoes, onions, and cilantro. As she discussed the nuances of the stock market, the life of a commuter in New York, her old neighbors, and the pain of being away from family, she peeled, chopped, diced, and assembled the salad, which went into a large glass bowl. A mortar and pestle—produced from under the table no less—was used to pound salted roasted peanuts, which then went into the salad. A squeeze of lime juice, a pinch of salt, and it was ready. She covered it and set it in the refrigerator to chill. I must have been staring. Self-consciously she apologized. "I am not a cookbook author like you," she said, "I just make these simple dishes. I hope you will like them."

The men returned and we began discussing the price of real estate in New York, a topic that never seems to go out of style. The tempting smell of tempering garlic and red chiles on the lentils brought us to the table, ravenous.

In the dining room, Vrinda had laid out traditional large steel plates and shining steel bowls for all of us. Indian-made steel glasses, filled with ice water, glistened with condensed droplets on the outside.

Tempered lentils, cumin rice, mustard potatoes, homemade yogurt, peanut salad, and of course two types of pickles were lunch that day. We were about to start when she appeared from the kitchen, apron covered in dusted flour, carrying hot *chapatis* (Indian griddle breads) doused with homemade *ghee* (clarified butter) on a platter.

We ate with quiet reverence. Her table with the simple dishes and well-worn tableware and her repeated insistences that we take seconds, reminded me of my grandmother's dinners.

Vrinda would disappear every few bites to roast more breads and then reappear, sweaty and yet ever hospitable. Her ingredients seemed to have fallen head over heels in love with one another. The (now) empty serving dishes vouched for it.

The meal was over and we moved to the living room. The shades were drawn to keep out the blistering August sun. The luxurious cool breeze of the air conditioner dared the heat of the summer sun. The room smelled of homemade bliss. We sat still embracing the peacefulness of the moment.

I turned to her and said, "I thought you said you can't cook?"

"I can't cook," she said nonchalantly. "This is a simple homemade meal. This is not really cooking. You should see the way my friends cook such lavish meals with gourmet curries and breads, exotic vegetables. Now that is real cooking."

But you can cook, I thought as I looked around at the contented faces. This, my dear friend, *is* real cooking.
❋

V's P's

These are the potatoes Vrinda served at lunch.

. . . .

1. In a large lidded skillet, heat the oil over medium heat. When the oil begins to shimmer, add the mustard seeds. When the seeds begin to crackle, add the red chiles.

2. Add the garlic and potatoes and sauté for 3 to 4 minutes.

3. Add the turmeric and mix well. Add the curry leaves and cilantro. Mix well and cook for another minute.

4. Add salt to taste and about 2 tablespoons of water. Cover and cook over low heat until the potatoes are tender, 12 to 15 minutes. Serve hot.

SERVE *4*

PREP/COOK TIME:
20 minutes

2 tablespoons vegetable oil
1 teaspoon black mustard seeds
4 whole dried red chiles
3 garlic cloves, crushed
1 pound baby potatoes, peeled and quartered
½ teaspoon ground turmeric
8 to 10 fresh curry leaves
2 tablespoons minced cilantro
Table salt

SERVES *4*

PREP/COOK TIME:

45 minutes

4 Anaheim peppers

1 tablespoon vegetable oil

1 teaspoon cumin seeds

¼ teaspoon ground
    turmeric (see Note)

1½ cups grated paneer

3 tablespoons heavy
    cream

Table salt

1 tablespoon minced
    cilantro

1 tablespoon Mint-
    Cilantro Chutney
    (page 36)

ANAHEIM PEPPERS WITH PANEER AND MINT-CILANTRO CHUTNEY

A friend of my father used to make deep-fried chiles stuffed with seasoned potatoes. I don't quite remember the variety of chile pepper that he used, but have found that Anaheim peppers remind me of the taste. Anaheim peppers do require some prep work but it is so simple—just broil them to remove the skin. Really, the peppers do all the hard work!

. . . .

1. To prepare the peppers, turn on the broiler to high. Place the peppers on a foil-lined baking sheet. Place them 3 to 4 inches away from the broiler and broil for 6 minutes on each side or until the skin of the peppers is beginning to blacken. Turn off the broiler. Remove the peppers with tongs and place them in a large bowl and cover the bowl with a plastic wrap. Let the peppers steam for about 15 minutes. When the peppers are cool enough to handle, gently remove and discard the skin. The peppers are very delicate at this point, so handle with care. Keeping the stem and tip intact, slit the peppers lengthwise. Using a small teaspoon, scoop out and discard all the seeds. Place the peppers, slit side up, back on the foil-lined sheet in a single layer.

2. Preheat oven to 350°F.

3. Heat the oil in a small saucepan on medium heat. When the oil begins to shimmer, add the cumin seeds. As soon as the cumin seeds sizzle, add the turmeric, paneer, cream, and salt to taste. Mix well and remove from the heat. Mix in the cilantro. Allow the mixture to come to room temperature.

4. Stuff each pepper with about a tablespoon of the paneer mixture, being careful that the cheese does not fall out.

5. Bake for 12 to 15 minutes, until the cheese has heated through and the sides of the pepper are just beginning to brown.

6. Serve immediately, drizzled with the chutney.

Note: Turmeric stains countertops and plastic containers. I have had people e-mail me with all kinds of solutions—bleach-based cleansers, Mr. Clean's Magic Eraser, Lysol. Be sure to try a little bit of the cleaner first to make sure it does not damage the countertop in any way.

Counting Peas

As a very young child, my son Jai had an unaccountable aversion to learning any language other than English. Yet I was determined to teach him Hindi, my mother tongue, to ensure he did not miss out on a culture and heritage for lack of simple knowledge of its language.

I would point to his clothes, toys, and books and encourage him to respond with their Hindi names. Eventually, he spoke a few words—he could point to a chair and call it *kursi* and say the numbers from one to ten in Hindi. But he did not know simple phrases such as "How are you?" or "My name is Jai." He could not have a conversation in Hindi.

That all changed during a trip to India when Jai was four. I was sitting with my mother on the floor, shelling peas. As we were laughing and talking, Jai wandered over, picked up a pea pod with great curiosity and asked what it was. It is *mattar*, my mother told him. Peas? he wondered. Inside this? He loved the fact that he could open the pod and find a treasure. He opened one, then an-

other and another. He sat still, which in itself was an achievement. He began to listen to us, to ask questions.

Some mothers like to color with their young children, some read books, some watch television. I could never have imagined our time together would be used to shell peas.

Once we were back in the States, I searched supermarkets and farmers' markets for peas in pods. I rinsed them, patted them dry, and waited for three o'clock so I could pick up Jai from school and we could shell peas. When pea pods were hard to find, I cheated, more than once passing off edamame as peas. Rarely were we able to eat the peas for dinner; by the time Jai's tiny fingers got them out of the pods, they were too squished or had gone straight into his mouth. I didn't care as long as we sat and shelled and talked.

We sat on the floor and started by sorting the pea pods, his fingers working furiously to separate the little baby pods from the mother pods and the daddy pods. Some days we named the piles of pods for his school friends—Zack, Sam, Casey. Then we counted. Jai could count to twenty in Hindi by then, and finished counting in English. On a few occasions, we reached thirty together.

Then came Jai's favorite part, the time for me to tell him stories—in Hindi. We always started with the story of the witch, the one who would come and make a home in your hair if you went out without drying it on a cold day. The story would somehow segue into what Buzz Lightyear or Spider-Man would do if he found this witch. (An interesting question, since we could not find a bit of hair on either of their heads.) Each story had a different ending, depending on which action figure was stationed next to Jai for the afternoon.

After the witch would come the story of an Indian princess who lived in a golden castle. I wanted it to end with her marrying a handsome prince. My son, however, would add his four-year-old's spin and American viewpoints. Sometimes the princess would be a doctor, usually a veterinarian, and would end up mar-

rying Shrek. Other times, the gentle princess would be transformed into a superhero and I was pleasantly challenged to come up with the Hindi names for laser guns and robotic evildoers.

One day Jai asked me, "Mom, *apne kahania kaha see seekhi?*"

Where did I learn the stories? Why, from Bahenjee, of course.

By now Jai knew that word meant "older sister," and his curiosity was piqued since I had no older sister. She was not related to me, I explained. It was a term often used as a mark of respect for an older person. A distant relative by marriage, she lived in a quiet part of my *dadi's* house in Delhi. Dadi, my father's mother, lived in what most people refer to as an Indian bungalow that housed a joint family—fourteen people on an average day, not including the various relatives who would show up out of the blue.

With her crooked teeth, thinning white hair, flowing white sari, and shrill voice, Bahenjee lived on the fringes of Dadi's household. She had her own small area—steel *almirah* (armoire), *charpai* (cot), and wildly painted and loud pictures of various gods on the mostly bare and peeling wall. On a shelf were statues of gods, incense sticks, fresh jasmine flowers, silver coins. Bahenjee generally rose at an ungodly hour, 4:00 a.m., and did the work of an alarm clock for the house, singing prayers tunelessly at the top of her voice.

"Ab who kaha hai?" asked Jai. Where is she now? I had no idea.

"Nanu se poochege?" He pointed to the phone for me to call his grandfather in India to ask him. I did, and my father told us that after my grandparents died, Bahenjee went to live with her son. She had since died.

Jai asked me more and more about her and her stories, and the memories came flooding back. On my summer vacations, when I was a child, I would look forward to going to Dadi's house so I could be with Bahenjee, for she was one of the best storytellers in the world. You and I shell peas, I told Jai; Bahenjee and I would make *sey* (noodles) as she shared stories. We would sit together in the hot Delhi sun after her ritual of sweeping the concrete courtyard with a wooden broomstick, brushing away dust and dirt I couldn't see, and laying out a bamboo mat, or *chitai*,

for us to sit on. She would spread newspapers in front of the mat and peel a few Indian oranges, *santras*, for me to eat. Then she would bring out the chickpea dough.

Bahenjee would make small logs of the dough, and she taught me how to hold each one between my fingers as if I were counting the beads of a rosary. Away we would go, preparing small bits of sev as princesses crossed paths with evil witches. Even as she talked, Bahenjee outpaced me in making sev. She would go through containers of dough while I was still struggling with my first log. She never seemed to notice that I generally made a mess and seemed to be interested only in the stories. Occasionally, she would ask me to wet a muslin cloth to cover the dough as it started to dry up. We would sit in that glowing Delhi heat for hours and I would listen, mesmerized.

As I recalled Bahenjee's stories for Jai, it occurred to me that the tales she had told me had been in Multani—I learned a dying language through her stories. All of the stories were set in my father's birthplace, Multan, a part of India until the separation of India and Pakistan. Bahenjee spoke Hindi, the more colloquial language, as well, but seemed to prefer telling the stories in her own language, stopping to translate only if I looked totally lost. She would recount painfully how she was forced to leave her motherland. She would talk about my father's childhood, about her own family, about the food and the festivities.

Her language connected me to a place I would never see and a culture I had never known. No one in my family ever returned to Multan. Bahenjee chronicled a history that was lost in a war over religion and hate. I learned prayers and nursery rhymes in Multani.

Bahenjee's stories ended, inevitably, when the dough did. I have always wondered what she did in the winter.

Learning to appreciate another culture through its language, through the words of an old woman who has seen life and lived to tell about it, now feels like a blessing. When my parents told us their childhood stories, we rolled our eyes. It always seemed to be intended as a lecture, prefaced with, "When I was your age . . ." Bahenjee's stories were different. They transported me, intrigued me.

Several years have gone by since Jai and I started counting peas. At the age of eight, he speaks Hindi, though not flawlessly. Often he mixes English and Hindi words to create his own language. He has even picked up a few stray words of Multani.

Now the questions he asks in his Hindi-English mix are no longer simple. "*Kya sab Iraqi log bad hai?*" Are all Iraqi people bad?

Why are those soldiers carrying *banndooks* (guns)?

Why do people die, will I die? *Aap bhi*? Will you?

Jai no longer struggles with the language; now it's my turn. I struggle for the right words, the right answers, in any language. ❊

JAI'S PEAS CURRY

SERVE 4

PREP/COOK TIME:

35 minutes, mostly unattended

2 tablespoons ghee or
   vegetable oil
1 small yellow onion,
   finely minced
¼ cup water
⅛ teaspoon ground cloves
¼ teaspoon ground
   cinnamon
1 cup fresh fenugreek
   leaves or ½ cup packed
   frozen, thawed
1 teaspoon dried
   fenugreek leaves
1 cup frozen peas, cooked
   and drained
1 cup frozen corn kernels,
   cooked and drained
1 cup heavy cream
¼ cup milk
Table salt
¼ teaspoon sugar

1. In a medium skillet, heat the ghee or oil over medium heat. Add the onion and sauté for 5 to 7 minutes, until the onion just begins to change color.

2. Add about ¼ cup water and cook for another 5 to 7 minutes, until the water has almost completely evaporated. Add the cloves, cinnamon, and both kinds of fenugreek. Sauté for 3 to 5 minutes, until the fenugreek leaves begin to wilt.

3. Add the peas, corn, cream, and milk. Reduce the heat to medium-low and bring the curry to a very gentle simmer. Reduce the heat to low.

4. Simmer for about 15 minutes or until the curry is thickened and fragrant. Add salt to taste and the sugar. Mix well.

5. Serve hot.

POULTRY, MEAT, and EGGS

. . . .

Several years ago I wrote an article for the *Washington Post* that tried to answer the question: "What is a chicken curry?" The article came about because I would constantly get e-mails from people asking for a chicken curry recipe. Well, as Chef Manjit Singh Gill of Bukhara, at the Maurya Sheraton in New Delhi, once told me, "Unlike other cuisines, India does not have specific recipes—we have guidelines. For instance, we all know what a curry should be like, something in a spiced sauce, but each area will put its spin on it, in fact each house will put its spin on it and what comes out the other end will still be a very specific curry." I love that insight. It is the same here in the United States. Barbecue in Texas or North Carolina or Kansas is unique and within these states every restaurant and home will add a unique twist.

Contrary to popular perception, Indians eat chicken, lamb, and yes, even beef. Religion, geography, availability, and even the influence of royalty help determine the use and preparation of meats. Catholics in south India eat beef, which is considered sacred in the north. I lived in a hostel with semicloistered nuns in the southern part of India, and they served me beef for the four years that I spent there. North Indian curries, rich in nuts and cream, derive their origins from the Muslim leaders who once held power there. In the subtropical south, curries incorporate coconut in every form, and in the eastern part of India the curries are simmered or steamed in mustard.

For my *Washington Post* article, I used friends, the phone book, Indian organizations, and the online food community eGullet.org to ask: "How do *you* make chicken curry?" You guessed it. I got many different recipes and methods, all of them rich in history and stories.

The recipes presented here are high in flavor and easy to prepare. I have tried to provide modern renditions of recipes that allow you to play with spices and produce delicious meals without slaving in the kitchen!

GREEN CHUTNEY CHICKEN

This recipe gets its inspiration from a green chile chicken dish that the chefs at the Bombay Club in Washington, D.C., prepare. The basic mint-cilantro chutney is supplemented with the flavor of bell peppers. The trick is to brown the chicken well, and only when the chicken is completely cooked add the aromatic herbal chutney. Don't overcook it or the sauce will lose its bright green color and turn a nasty brown!

I like to serve this with basmati rice.

. . . .

1. Put the chutney, bell pepper, and water into a blender and process until smooth. Set aside.

2. In a nonstick skillet, heat the oil over medium heat. When it begins to shimmer, add the ginger-garlic paste and sauté for about 1 minute.

3. Add the chicken and cook over medium-high heat for 12 to 15 minutes, until well browned and cooked through.

4. Add the chutney mixture and salt to taste. Bring to a gentle simmer and immediately remove from the heat.

5. Garnish with the green chiles and serve immediately.

SERVES 4
PREP/COOK TIME:
20 minutes

1 cup Mint-Cilantro Chutney (page 36)
1 organic green bell pepper, seeded and roughly chopped (see Note, page 123)
¼ cup water
2 tablespoons vegetable oil
1 tablespoon store-bought ginger-garlic paste
1½ pounds skinless, boneless chicken, cut into 1-inch cubes
Table salt
2 green serrano chiles, slit and seeded (page 144), for garnish

INDIAN-STYLE CHILI
IN BREAD BOWLS

Serves 4

Prep/Cook time:
50 minutes

2 tablespoons vegetable
oil
1 cinnamon stick
1 medium red onion,
minced
1 tablespoon store-bought
ginger-garlic paste
One 14.5-ounce can fire-
roasted diced tomatoes
or 2 large tomatoes,
diced
1¼ pounds ground beef or
ground turkey
½ teaspoon red chile
powder
¼ teaspoon ground
turmeric
¼ teaspoon ground
cinnamon
⅛ teaspoon ground cloves
½ teaspoon ground
coriander

*S*erved in sourdough bread bowls, this chili makes a hearty meal. My son loves this after an arduous soccer game. Traditionally, this is served with griddle breads but I prefer it in a bread bowl. Either way, garnish with finely chopped onions and green chiles. This recipe works well with ground turkey, giving the usually bland turkey meat a nice spiciness.

. . . .

1. In a large lidded skillet, heat the vegetable oil over medium-high heat. When the oil begins to shimmer, add the cinnamon stick. When the stick begins to sizzle, add the onion and ginger-garlic paste. Sauté, stirring, until the onion is golden brown, 7 to 8 minutes. Add a few tablespoons of water if the onion starts to stick to the pan.

2. Add the tomatoes. Cook for about 15 minutes or until the oil begins to leave the sides of the mixture.

3. Add the beef and cook for 10 to 12 minutes, breaking up the meat with a spatula.

4. Add the chile powder, turmeric, cinnamon, cloves, and coriander. Mix well. Cook for about 2 minutes.

5. Add the kidney beans and 1½ cups water. Cover and cook for another 12 to 15 minutes, until the beef is cooked through.

6. While the chili is cooking, prepare the bread bowls: Cut ½ inch off the top of each loaf. Gently scoop out the bread from inside the loaf, using care to leave a generous ¾-inch shell intact.

7. Once the chili is cooked, remove the cinnamon stick, spoon a cupful of chili into each bowl, salt to taste, garnish with onion and chiles (if using), and serve immediately.

One 15- to 16-ounce can red kidney beans, drained

1½ cups water

Four 1-pound round loaves sourdough bread at least 5 inches across

Table salt

Finely chopped onion and green chiles (optional) for garnish

TAMARIND CHICKEN

SERVES *4*

PREP/COOK TIME:
15 minutes

2 tablespoons vegetable
   oil
2 or 3 medium or 6 to 8
   small organic shallots,
   sliced
3 small green serrano
   chiles, slit lengthwise
1 garlic clove, sliced thin
1 pound chicken strips,
   cut into 1-inch cubes
½ teaspoon ground
   turmeric
½ teaspoon red chile
   flakes
Table salt
1 tablespoon store-bought
   tamarind-date chutney

This stir-fry is great on top of steamed basmati rice. I use a tablespoon of prepared tamarind chutney to add a quick tamarind flavor to this dish.

. . . .

1. Heat the oil in a medium skillet over high heat. When the oil beings to shimmer, add the shallots and green chiles. Sauté for about 1 minute or until the shallots just begin to change color.

2. Add the garlic and sauté for another 30 seconds.

3. Add the chicken and cook 7 to 8 minutes, until the chicken is cooked through.

4. Add the turmeric, chile flakes, and salt to taste, and cook for another minute. Add the tamarind chutney and mix until the spice mixture has coated the chicken well. Remove from the heat. Serve hot.

WHOLE ROAST CHICKEN WITH FENUGREEK

I learned to roast chicken whole from my culinary hero, Mark Bittman. I love his no-fuss method of roasting. I don't truss a small chicken, but any larger bird will need to be trussed. Please use butter if you want a crisp skin on the chicken; oil just does not work the same way.

. . . .

1. Preheat the oven to 450°F. Remove the chicken giblets and cut off any excess fat. Rinse the chicken and pat it dry—do this well or the moisture will produce steam when you roast it. Salt and pepper the inside cavity of the chicken. Place the chicken on a rack in a large roasting pan.

2. In a bowl combine the softened butter, 1 teaspoon each salt and pepper, the chile flakes, and fenugreek leaves. Rub this mixture liberally all over the chicken, making sure you work your fingers under the skin, as well.

3. Roast the chicken breast side down for 20 to 30 minutes, until the skin begins to brown. Baste it and turn breast side up.

4. Baste the breast, which should be starting to brown. Cook for 5 minutes.

5. Baste again and now reduce the temperature to 325°F. Roast for another 45 to 55 minutes, until the juices run clear. For a very well-browned chicken, you can place it under a hot broiler, for a few minutes before taking it out of the oven.

6. Remove the chicken from the oven and place on a platter. Allow it to rest for about 10 minutes. Carve and serve. If you wish, drizzle the pan juices over the carved chicken.

SERVES *4 to 6*

PREP/COOK TIME: *About 1 hour and 40 minutes, mostly unattended*

One 3- to 4-pound whole chicken
4 tablespoons unsalted butter, softened
1 teaspoon table salt
1 teaspoon freshly ground black pepper
1 teaspoon red chile flakes
2 tablespoons dried fenugreek leaves, crushed
Melted butter for basting

CHICKEN WITH MINT AND GINGER RUB

Serves 4

Prep/Cook time:

35 minutes plus 20 minutes to refrigerate

1 tablespoon dried mint
1 teaspoon red chile flakes
¼ teaspoon turmeric
½ teaspoon carom seeds
1 teaspoon grated peeled
   fresh ginger
¼ teaspoon freshly
   ground black pepper
½ teaspoon ground cumin
¼ teaspoon table salt to
   start
¼ cup heavy cream
1¼ pounds skinless,
   boneless chicken
   thighs, each cut into
   two pieces
Nonstick cooking spray
Sliced red onions for
   garnish

int is highly aromatic and very flavorful. It is a really easy way to add zing to bland chicken. Serve this chicken by itself or over dark greens like steamed or sautéed spinach for a full meal. This is a very versatile recipe—play with the rub, substituting dried fenugreek for the mint or crushed fennel seeds for the ginger. The possibilities are endless and delicious!

. . . .

1. In a bowl or resealable plastic bag, combine the mint, chile flakes, turmeric, carom seeds, ginger, pepper, cumin, salt, and cream. Mix well. Add the chicken and coat well. Refrigerate for 20 minutes.

2. Preheat the oven to 400°F. Line a baking sheet with foil and spray it generously. Place the chicken on the baking sheet in a single layer. Discard any remaining marinade.

3. Roast for 20 to 30 minutes, until the chicken is completely cooked through. Serve hot, garnished with the sliced red onions.

Au Contraire

·······································

I grew up in the Middle East, away from my home country of India. Every summer when we visited home, the first thing my grandma served all the visiting grandkids was a tiny bit of her favorite drink. My sari-wearing Indian grandmother (who was as traditional as they come) was in love, totally in love with Campa Cola (an Indian version of a soda). On the day of our arrival, she would summon her servant and tell him, "All the kids are here, now go and get some really cold Campa and don't add any ice. Put a little in the small steel glasses for the kids." We all knew this was a once-a-vacation treat and would enjoy it tremendously as she joined us, and we laughed and shared stories with her of the year gone by. Recently, when I shared this with a friend, her reaction struck me as odd. "Your grandma let you drink cola? My parents used to keep the soda under lock and key." We did not grow up drinking super-sized drinks, I tried to tell her; an old lady indulged her grandkids with a four-ounce glass of cola—

since when is that bad? I hesitated to tell her more as I wondered what her reaction would be to my other memories: Mom waiting at the door with "midnight beauties," a touch of Coke in a glass topped with vanilla ice cream when I came home from school after a tough test; Dad and I decorating my birthday cake with M&Ms; or my other grandma showing me how to deep-fry breads.

Dinner in my paternal grandmother's house was served in the large dining/living/TV/all-in-one room on a *chitai* (a large floor mat). All the food was placed in the center and the entire clan—about fifteen of us on a good day—would sit cross-legged on the floor and eat. Dadi could not sit on the floor due to her health and would sit on a couch on the side. She would ask the servant to bring the piping hot rotis, gently rubbed with homemade ghee that he would make fresh as we would sit down to eat. She would place each one on her hand. Then she would close her hand and gently crush the rotis in her fist to break them up a bit. She always said it softens them for her children (her children being close to forty-plus at this time!). From my father, her oldest son, to my youngest cousin, her one-year-old grandson, everyone would wait for those rotis that were enveloped with such love. She would always say that we should eat everything in moderation, "I know you love rotis, but eat more than two and you will get a tummy ache." I use ghee, which has wrongly been given the status of bad for you, when I serve rice or rotis to my kids today—just a touch to add taste and flavor. I love a bit of ghee in my food—a touch . . .

My grandmothers died when I was young but I recall spending many hours with them chopping vegetables, peeling oranges, or shelling peanuts. There was never a question of whether we did or did not like to eat these things. They prepared dinner and we ate it. Simple as that. And we loved it.

My mother, continuing in the tradition of my grandmothers, never hid vegetables from us, either; no, there was never any squash puree in our sweets. She may have sneaked some into our turnovers but always in a way that when I saw a pea, it looked like a pea. She taught me not just how to cook but how to eat—how to bite into a ripe guava, how to open a luscious lychee, how to puree a watermelon, how to peel pea pods, how to tell a ripe lemon, how to suck on a whole mango, how to roast cumin, how to sizzle mustard seeds in smoking oil, how to smell fresh cilantro—always encouraging me to smell, scrutinize, and taste what was in our kitchen and on our table.

My mother wasn't a very adventurous cook but my father, well, he was a gourmet. A well-traveled man, he would come home with stories of Jordanian sumac, tales of Swedish rosti, tastes of Parisian pastries, chronicles of German beer tastings, and always boxes of Lindt chocolates. He introduced my palate to tastes of the world, with only one line of advice: Just try it once.

I have tried to pass on the same love and understanding of food to my son. His godmother, Janet, loves to bake and share cookies with him. He comes to the market to help me buy vegetables, and when we puree beets to add to his pancake batter, he knows it and sees it. I don't lock up the soda. I make him the same floats my mother did. Once a month, we enjoy them together. I think being open and honest about what we are eating and acknowledging that indulgences are not only fun to eat but good for your culinary soul is a nurturing way to raise kids. My son is old enough to read food labels—no trans fat, he says, when choosing cereals. He can tell ginger from garlic and he can smell cilantro from a mile away.

He loves a touch of ghee on his Indian bread. I know my grandma would be proud. ❊

RED CHILE, GARLIC, AND BASIL CHICKEN

SERVES *4*

PREP/COOK TIME:
40 minutes

1 tablespoon vegetable oil

5 medium or 8 to 10 small
organic shallots, sliced

4 or 5 garlic cloves, sliced

3 dried red chiles, roughly
pounded

½ teaspoon ground
turmeric

¼ teaspoon table salt

1½ pounds skinless,
boneless, chicken
thighs, cubed

¼ cup water

8 to 10 basil leaves

½ of a 13.5-ounce can
coconut milk
(optional)

Basil has been used in India for several hundred years. I have yet to find Indian basil here in the United States, so I use Thai basil or regular Italian basil. I tried to grow Indian basil and it worked for one season but alas, no more.

This is a very easy stir-fry, just perfect on nights when you have ten minutes to get dinner on the table. Serve this with steamed white or brown basmati rice. You can adjust the heat to your taste.

. . . .

1. In a large lidded skillet, heat the oil over medium heat. Add the shallots and garlic and cook for 3 to 4 minutes until the garlic begins to change color.

2. Add the chiles, turmeric, and salt. Sauté for 1 minute.

3. Add the chicken pieces and sauté for about 10 minutes. Add about ¼ cup of water, cover, and cook for about 15 minutes, until the chicken is done.

4. Add the basil leaves, mix well. Remove from the heat and serve hot.

If you prefer a curry with your chicken, add a half can of coconut milk in step 3 and allow it to simmer for about 20 minutes.

Did you know . . . Indian basil or *tulsi* is a plant that is considered sacred and is worshipped in India?

CHICKEN BREASTS STUFFED WITH PANEER

$\mathcal{I}$ learned the art of stuffing chicken breasts from watching one of my all-time favorite TV chefs, Ina Garten. I love the way her food is simple yet uses powerful flavors and fresh ingredients. I use her technique here to stuff the breasts. So here's to Ina, with many thanks!

. . . .

1. Preheat the oven to 375°F. Line a baking sheet with foil and grease it with cooking spray.

2. In a small bowl, combine the butter, ginger-garlic paste, and 1 teaspoon salt. Loosen the skin from the breasts with your fingers, leaving one side attached. Rub the paste all over the chicken breasts. Set aside.

3. In another bowl combine the paneer, green chiles, cilantro, turmeric, chile powder, and ¼ teaspoon salt. Mix well.

4. Stuff this filling into the pocket between the skin and the meat, dividing it evenly among the chicken breasts.

5. Place the breasts on the baking sheet. Bake the breasts for 35 to 40 minutes, until just cooked through. Baste with butter half way through.

6. Serve hot or at room temperature.

$\mathcal{D}$i∂ you know . . . paneer is not a cheese that melts, yet it tastes amazing when baked.

Nonstick cooking spray

1 tablespoon unsalted butter, melted, plus extra for basting

1 tablespoon store-bought ginger-garlic paste

1¼ teaspoons table salt

4 bone-in, skin-on chicken breast halves

1 cup finely grated paneer

2 small green serrano chiles, minced

2 tablespoons minced cilantro

¼ teaspoon ground turmeric

1 teaspoon red chile powder or red chile flakes

STIR-FRIED LAMB

SERVES *4*

PREP/COOK TIME:

40 minutes, mostly unattended

2 tablespoons vegetable oil

1 teaspoon cumin seeds

1 teaspoon fennel seeds

1 tablespoon coriander
   seeds, crushed

1 green cardamom pod
   (see Note)

4 whole cloves

1 small red onion, thinly
   sliced

2 teaspoons store-bought
   ginger-garlic paste

1 pound boneless lean
   lamb (leg of lamb),
   diced into 1-inch cubes

5 or 6 small green serrano
   chiles, slit lengthwise

¼ teaspoon ground turmeric

1 dried red chile, broken
   into 2 to 3 pieces
   (optional)

½ teaspoon table salt to start

¼ cup slivered unsweetened
   coconut or coconut pieces
   (see page 23; optional)

1 tablespoon fresh lemon
   juice or white vinegar

¼ cup water

My cousin Dimple taught me how to make this. It is an unusual way to cook lamb, but I find the vinegar and warming spices complement the lamb perfectly. Serve with steamed rice.

. . . .

1. In a large lidded skillet heat the oil over medium heat. When the oil shimmers, add the cumin, fennel, coriander, cardamom, and cloves. When the spices begin to sizzle, add the onion. Sauté the onion for 5 to 6 minutes, until it begins to soften and change color.

2. Add the ginger-garlic paste, the lamb, and green chiles. Increase the heat to high. Cook the lamb, stirring constantly, for 6 to 7 minutes, until the lamb is well browned.

3. Add the turmeric, red chile (if using), ½ teaspoon salt, coconut, lemon juice, and about ¼ cup water. Lower the heat to medium.

4. Cover and cook for about 20 minutes, until the lamb is completely cooked.

5. Uncover and cook over high heat until most of the liquid dries up and the lamb begins to crisp. Salt to taste.

6. Serve immediately.

Note: The cardamom used in this book is green or black cardamom, as the recipes specify. Some Indian stores sell white cardamom. It is basically green cardamom pods that are bleached white—I am not sure why!

CORIANDER-AND-FENNEL CRUSTED LAMB CHOPS

This easy-to-prepare lamb dish is very flavorful and will make your kitchen smell great. Serve with a side of mint chutney and steamed vegetables.

. . . .

1. Trim fat from chops and place them in a flat dish.

2. In a small bowl, combine the garlic, ginger, coriander, fennel, chile, cardamom, salt, and oil. Sprinkle the mix over the chops and rub it in with your fingers which are the best tools to ensure that you cover each chop well and evenly.

3. Cover with plastic wrap and refrigerate for about 30 minutes.

4. Light spray a cast-iron grill pan and heat it over high heat until almost smoking. Add the chops and sear for about 2 minutes. Flip the chops over and cook for another 3 minutes for medium-rare or 3½ minutes for medium.

5. Allow the chops to rest for 5 minutes before serving.

4 lamb chops, cut 1-inch thick
1 garlic clove, minced
¼ teaspoon minced peeled fresh ginger
¾ teaspoon coriander seeds, crushed
½ teaspoon fennel seeds, crushed
1 dried red chile, broken into 2 to 3 pieces
Seeds from 1 green cardamom pod, pounded
¼ teaspoon table salt
1 tablespoon vegetable oil
Nonstick cooking spray

CURRIED EGG SALAD WITH CARAMELIZED ONION

SERVES *4 to 6*

PREP/COOK TIME:
20 minutes, including time to boil eggs

2 tablespoons vegetable oil

½ medium red onion, thinly sliced

¼ teaspoon table salt

½ teaspoon sugar

½ teaspoon freshly ground black pepper

6 hard-cooked eggs, peeled

¼ medium red onion, finely diced

½ medium red or orange organic bell pepper, seeded and finely diced (see Note, page 123)

¾ cup mayonnaise

2 tablespoons minced cilantro

1 small green serrano chile, minced

1½ teaspoons hot Madras curry powder

1 tablespoon prepared mustard

2 cups spinach leaves, loosely packed

*Y*es, I know, a typical American egg salad has no roots in any traditional Indian dish, anywhere! But I tell you, I have seen it in the homes of countless Indian friends here in the United States, and I would really be amiss if I did not mention it here. Eggs have always been used in Indian cooking, and the humble egg salad is the perfect example of how a dish from the West was "Indian-ized" and is in the repertoire of many young Indian home cooks today.

. . . .

1. Caramelize the onions: Heat the oil in a medium skillet over medium heat. Add the sliced onion and fry for about 5 minutes until it becomes transparent. Add ¼ teaspoon salt, the sugar, and the pepper and sauté for another minute. As soon as it changes color, remove from the heat and set aside until the rest of the salad is ready.

2. In a large bowl, mash the boiled eggs with a fork or finely chop them. Add the diced onion and bell pepper and mix well.

3. In a separate bowl, combine the mayonnaise, cilantro, chile, curry powder, and salt to taste. Mix well. Add the mustard and mix until well combined. Add to the eggs and mix.

4. Divide the spinach leaves onto four serving plates. Heap the egg salad evenly onto each plate. Top with the caramelized onions and serve.

BEEF STEWED WITH COCONUT

This was a staple dish for me during my engineering days in south India. I was lucky enough to be invited to the homes of friends whose mothers cooked this very mildly spiced dish. They served it with lacy rice and lentil pancakes. I make it for my kids often and they love to sop up the stew with just plain toasted bread! As I recall, this stew was made in a pressure cooker, but I use a Dutch oven and allow the stew to simmer, untouched, for an hour or so until it is cooked. If you want to give the dish a yellowish hue, you can add a teaspoon of turmeric. You can also add other vegetables here like winter squash or turnips at the point when you add the potatoes.

. . . .

1. In a deep lidded saucepan or Dutch oven, heat the oil over high heat. Add the onion, chile, coriander, salt, beef, and potatoes and fry for 5 to 7 minutes, until the meat begins to brown.

2. Add the water. Cover and cook for 10 to 12 minutes, until the stew begins to thicken.

3. Add the coconut milk. Cook for another 45 minutes, covered, over medium-low heat, until the meat is tender and completely cooked. If the stew dries up too much, you can add up to ½ cup of water. Adjust the salt here as the seasoning will change with the addition of water. I prefer my stew thick.

4. Drop in the curry leaves. Stir and serve.

Note: Chuck is a tough but flavorful meat that needs long, slow cooking.

SERVES 4

PREP/COOK TIME:
1¼ hours, mostly unattended

- 2 tablespoons vegetable oil
- 1 medium red onion, minced
- 1 small green serrano chile, minced
- 1 tablespoon ground coriander
- ¼ teaspoon table salt to start
- 1 pound boneless chuck, cut into 1-inch cubes (see Note)
- 2 small Idaho potatoes, peeled and diced
- 2½ cups water
- One 13.5-ounce can coconut milk
- Handful of fresh curry leaves

THE LEGENDARY CHICKEN 65

Serves *4*

Prep-Cook time: *20 minutes*

1 cup plain yogurt (such as Dannon)

2 tablespoons cornstarch

1 teaspoon store-bought ginger-garlic paste

1 teaspoon red chile powder or red chile flakes (or more)

1 tablespoon fresh lemon juice

2 drops red food coloring

¼ teaspoon table salt to start

1¼ pounds chicken tenders, cut into 2-inch cubes

2 cups plus 2 tablespoons vegetable oil

1 teaspoon black mustard seeds

4 small green serrano chiles, finely chopped

20 fresh curry leaves

A few years ago sitting at Swagath, a popular South Indian restaurant in South Delhi, I scanned the menu to see if they had Chicken 65. This is a deep-fried chicken dish that has always been a favorite of mine. I hunt for it wherever I go in India and generally it is available in some rendition or other. But why is it called Chicken 65? The stories that surround it are as fascinating as the dish itself. (To get an idea of how popular it is, Google the name and you will get over 50,000 hits and probably as many recipes!)

Depending on which version you believe, Chicken 65 gets its name—because the chicken used is sixty-five days old, from the sixty-five spices purportedly included, from its sixty-fifth place on a menu somewhere, or from the age of the chef who first prepared it. The claims are almost as many as the versions of the dish. The most likely source of the name is that the dish was number 65 on the menu of Buhari's Hotel on Mount Road in Madras (now known as Chennai), a bustling metropolis in South India. That's the explanation from Vikram Doctor, a journalist with the *Economic Times* who has actually eaten this at Buhari's many times. Its popularity in most Indian bars is credited to the truck drivers who enjoy the spicy dish along with their drinks.

So, back to Swagath. I scanned the menu and found it. It's the first thing I ordered along with a glass of fresh lime soda. The waiter smiled knowingly, "Madam, it is our most popular item." I smiled back. Encouraged, he continued, "Do you know it gets the name from being served at a truckers' stop near the sixty-fifth milestone outside Hyderabad?"

. . . .

1. In a large bowl, combine the yogurt, cornstarch, ginger-garlic paste, chile powder, lemon juice, food coloring, and salt. Mix well. Do not worry if the marinade looks pink! When you deep-fry the chicken it will turn a luscious reddish-brown. Add the chicken chunks and mix to combine.

2. Heat 2 cups of the oil in a deep fryer. When the oil is hot but not smoking, add a small piece of bread; if the bread floats to the top, the oil is ready. Add a few pieces of chicken at a time and fry until the chicken is crisp on the outside and cooked on the inside, 2 to 3 minutes. Remove the chicken using a slotted spoon and drain on a paper towel. Continue until you have fried all the pieces. Be sure to allow time between frying for the oil to reheat to the right temperature. Discard any remaining marinade.

3. Place the chicken on a serving platter.

4. In a small skillet, heat the remaining 2 tablespoons vegetable oil. When the oil begins to shimmer, add the mustard seeds. When the seeds begin to sizzle, add the green chiles and curry leaves. Fry for about 30 seconds, until the curry leaves begin to crisp. If you can handle the spice, add another ¼ teaspoon of chile powder to the oil just before removing it from the heat.

5. Pour over the chicken and serve.

INDIAN CHICKEN WINGS

Serves *6 to 8*

Prep/Cook time: *about 25 minutes, plus 3 hours marination*

1 cup heavy cream

1 tablespoons store-bought ginger-garlic paste

½ teaspoon ground turmeric

½ teaspoon ground cumin

1½ teaspoon ground coriander

2 teaspoons red chile flakes

2 tablespoons fresh lemon juice

1½ teaspoons dried fenugreek leaves, crushed

1 teaspoon dried mango powder

2 tablespoons vegetable oil

1½ teaspoons table salt

¼ teaspoon freshly ground black pepper

2½ pounds chicken wings (about 20 wings), tips cut off

Nonstick cooking spray

Store-bought chaat masala for garnish

ere's an American classic with a twist. These grilled wings provide all the flavor yet are healthier than their deep-fried cousins. I make these in bulk, as they freeze well. When you are ready, just throw them on the grill and get ready to party.

. . . .

1. In a large bowl, combine the cream, ginger-garlic paste, turmeric, cumin, coriander, chile flakes, lemon juice, fenugreek, mango powder, vegetable oil, salt, and pepper.

2. Add the chicken wings and toss to thoroughly coat them. Refrigerate, covered, for at least 3 hours.

3. Turn on the broiler to high. Line a baking sheet with foil and spray it lightly.

4. Place the wings on the baking sheet. Pour any remaining marinade on top of the wings.

5. Broil the wings about 4 inches from the heat until cooked through, about 12 minutes on each side or until they begin to brown well. Turn the wings once.

6. Serve sprinkled with chaat masala.

Chicken with a Guava Marinade

In India, curries made with guava are traditional though uncommon. *Amrood* (guava) is eaten raw, sprinkled with salt and lemon juice. I use it pureed as a marinade for chicken. Guava adds richness to this chicken dish. It is a simple marinade that does not require much fussing, but do use the best quality puree that you can find. That is what makes all the difference!

. . . .

1. In a large bowl, combine the guava puree, chile flakes, lemon and orange juices, honey, and ginger. Add the chicken and mix well. Cover and refrigerate for at least 1 hour.

2. Heat a large lidded skillet over medium heat. Add the chicken with its marinade. Cook on high heat for 3 to 5 minutes, until the chicken browns.

3. Cover and reduce the heat to low. Cook for 15 to 20 minutes, until the chicken is completely cooked through. The sauce will be relatively thin at this point.

4. Remove the cover and increase the heat to high. Cook until the sauce becomes very thick and clings to the chicken. Remove from the heat and serve immediately.

Serves 4
Prep/Cook time:
40 minutes plus 1 hour refrigeration

½ cup pink guava puree (see page 246)
1 teaspoon red chile flakes
1 tablespoon fresh lemon juice
1 tablespoon fresh orange juice
1 tablespoon liquid honey
½ teaspoon minced peeled fresh ginger
4 or 5 chicken drumsticks, skins removed and meat slit with a knife

FISH and SHELLFISH

. . . .

onsidering that India has 4,300 miles of coastline, is it any surprise that succulent freshwater fish, scores of saltwater fish, king crabs, tiger prawns, lobsters, mussels, clams, oysters, scallops—an almost endless list—are found on the Indian table? Most people find this to be surprising. I was eating at an Indian restaurant in Fairfax, Virginia, that served a spicy mussel stew. Another Indian patron sitting next to me was haranguing the waiter, "Why are you people always trying to copy the western world and adding mussels to your menu? Why all this fusion?" It isn't fusion. Mussels have been a staple in Kerala, a southern Indian state, for years.

Indian coastlines have not only been blessed with abundant seafood, but have also been the recipients of cooking techniques, ingredients, and the knowledge of traders from far-flung places. All of this makes the preparation of Indian fish dishes as diverse as the continent itself. The western coastline of India was influenced in large part by Christianity and Islam, while the eastern coastline reflects the rich cuisines of Sri Lanka, China, and Malaysia.

A large part of the Indian coastline also boasts luscious coconut palms, and hence the use of coconut in the cooking of fish is predominant. Sweet, sour, salty, spicy—all of these tastes show up in Indian seafood recipes. Some fish are

173

sweetened with jaggery (cane sugar), some are spiked with pickles, others come alive with peppers, and yet others are dunked in velvety smooth coconut curries. The cooking methods are just as varied—fried, sautéed, deep-fried, broiled, steamed, baked—the list is never-ending. Marry this with the lush lagoons, emerald hills, sun-drenched beaches, and tranquil backwaters, and you have a formula that gives the cuisine in these regions a vivacity that matches India and its people.

Let's start our journey along the coastline of India, beginning with the western coast. The Parsi community of western India has contributed the almost legendary *patra ni macchi* (pomfret steamed in banana leaves). The Goan community reflects its Portuguese heritage in its famed fish curries and spicy preparations of *tessryo* (baby clams). The Hindu Mangalorians offer fiery recipes with crabs. The Konkan Café and Mahesh Fish House in Mumbai are a couple of the classic restaurants offering these delightful dishes. In the southern state of Andhra Pradesh, everything is hot. Spiced to the hilt with its famed *assampati* chile, the fish dishes here are not for the faint-hearted.

The cuisine of the Chettiars or Chettinand is so famous, the U.S.-based restaurant chain Legal Sea Foods serves Fish Chettinand on its regular menu. (The Chettiars were merchants and traders on the eastern coast of India.)

Moving to the eastern coastline, the golden state of Bengal is probably the jewel in India's fish cookery crown. Famed for their love and sometimes reverence for fish, the Bengalis are very particular about which fish they will eat and how it is prepared. Their unique method of marinating fish in yogurt is now world famous.

Of course, inland India is not far behind, either. The tasty fried fish from the holy city of Amritsar, the baked trout from Kashmir, or the dried fish *ka salaam* (curry) from the landlocked Hyderabad mark the genius of the chefs and cooks of these areas.

Chef-extraordinaire Ananada Solomon told me once: "Seafood preparations in India until today depended on what time of year you are talking about, since the recipes use the ingredients and fish available at that time of the year. In the monsoon season most folks here, in Mumbai, eat dried fish (since commercial fishing during the monsoons is not possible). However, in the Konkan coast you will see local fisherman with special nets trying to fish in the heavy rain, so even in the monsoon season they will have some fresh fish for home consumption."

Referred to by the Indian media as the Versace of Indian cuisine, Solomon has single-handedly made coastal Indian cooking a household delight. His restaurant at the Taj President hotel in Mumbai focuses on the best of west coast food. He was the first Indian to be selected to represent the country at the World Gourmet Summit held each April in Singapore. In his restaurant kitchen is an old Indian woman from his village. Her sole job is to grind the spices for him in a specific way.

Indian seafood is starting to gain popularity in Indian restaurants abroad. In general, outside of India, many North Indian restaurants stayed focused on Mughlai cuisine, concentrating on the traditional meats and poultry rather than seafood. The South Indian restaurants have focused primarily on the vegetarian cuisine of the south. But as people become more sophisticated in their tastes and their desire for true ethnic food, a major change is brewing. The best kept secret of India is out, and fish dishes are finding a place on Indian menus everywhere. Gone are the days when Goan fish curry was the sole claim to fish fame on Indian menus. Menus are being adorned with the true jewels of Indian cooking; shrimp stir-fried with curry leaves, mussels stewed in coconut milk, chile squid, and scallops in coconut milk are some examples of this trend.

CHILE SQUID

SERVES 4

PREP/COOK TIME:

15 minutes

2 tablespoons vegetable
   oil
¼ large red onion, diced
20 fresh curry leaves
1 pound calamari rings,
   rinsed and patted dry
   (see Note)
1 teaspoon red chile flakes
½ teaspoon turmeric
1½ teaspoons store-
   bought hot Madras
   curry powder
About ½ teaspoon table
   salt
Fresh lemon juice

The secret to making sure this simple recipe turns out great is to serve it hot right off the stove. My husband swears that the quantity of chile in the squid is directly proportional to my mood of the hour!

. . . .

1. Heat the vegetable oil in a medium skillet over high heat until almost smoking. Add the onion, curry leaves, and calamari rings and cook for about 4 to 5 minutes, until the calamari is cooked through and begins to brown very lightly.

2. Add the chile flakes, turmeric, curry powder, and salt and cook for another 3 to 4 minutes, until the spices are well mixed in with the calamari.

3. Remove from the heat. Squeeze a few drops of fresh lemon juice on the calamari and serve immediately.

Note: I buy my calamari rings from my local Korean fish store. It sells them cleaned and frozen in a bag. That makes them very easy to use and store, and saves the cleaning time and mess.

FISH FRY

*f*ried fish is an English favorite, but this version meets my unrelenting passion for spicier flavors. A bit of red chile, a pinch of turmeric—and this old classic has a new look and a superb taste to match. This simple-to-prepare dish is crispy and delicious. One tip here: If you refrigerate the fillets for a few minutes before you fry, it will help the coating adhere.

. . . .

1. Make a paste of the lemon juice, chile powder, turmeric, ginger, pepper, salt, green chiles, and cornstarch. Rub the paste on the fish with your fingers. Cover and chill for 10 to 20 minutes.

2. Heat the oil in a large skillet, over medium heat. When the oil begins to shimmer, add the fish and cook for 3 to 4 minutes on each side, until completely cooked through. (Cook a minute or so longer if you like the outside of the fish to be extra crispy.)

3. Transfer to a paper towel to drain.

4. Serve immediately with Mint-Cilantro Chutney.

SERVES *2*

PREP/COOK TIME: *about 10 minutes hands-on, plus 20 minutes to chill*

2 tablespoons fresh lemon juice

½ teaspoon red chile powder

¼ teaspoon ground turmeric

1 teaspoon minced peeled fresh ginger

¼ teaspoon freshly ground black pepper

¼ teaspoon table salt

2 or 3 small green serrano chiles, finely minced

1 teaspoon cornstarch

2 small fillets white fish such as tilapia, about ½ pound total

1 tablespoon vegetable oil

Mint-Cilantro Chutney (page 36) for serving

CURRIED SCALLOPS

SERVES 4

PREP/COOK TIME:

30 minutes plus 10 minutes marination

1 pound sea scallops
(about 12)

1 tablespoon mild curry
powder

4 tablespoons vegetable
oil, divided

½ teaspoon black mustard
seeds

8 fresh curry leaves

1 teaspoon grated peeled
fresh ginger

½ medium red onion,
minced

¼ teaspoon table salt

½ teaspoon red chile
powder

¼ teaspoon ground
turmeric

One 13.5-ounce can
coconut milk

These are perfectly seared scallops with the warmth of Indian curry powder. I read somewhere that scallops should be seared on one side and just gently kissed on the other—this really does describe the best way to prepare these.

. . . .

1. Place the scallops in a bowl and rub them with the curry powder. Set aside for about 10 minutes.

2. In a large nonstick skillet, heat 2 tablespoons of the vegetable oil on high heat. When the oil is shimmering and almost smoking, add the scallops. Cook in batches if necessary to avoid crowding the pan. Sear on one side for about 2 minutes. Flip and continue to cook until cooked through and opaque. (Tongs work well for flipping.) Transfer to a paper towel to drain. Continue until all the scallops are fried.

3. In the same skillet, heat the remaining 2 tablespoons of vegetable oil. Add the mustard seeds. When they sputter add the curry leaves, ginger, and onion. Sauté for 4 to 5 minutes, until the onion is well browned.

4. Reduce the heat to medium. Add the salt, chile powder, and turmeric and sauté for another minute. Add the coconut milk and simmer on low for about 10 minutes. Don't let the coconut milk boil.

5. Return the scallops to the curry and simmer for another 5 minutes or until they are completely heated through. Serve hot.

POMEGRANATE SHRIMP

SERVES *4 as an entree*
PREP/COOK TIME:
15 minutes

This dish cooks in just a few minutes. Don't overcook the shrimp or they will become rubbery—remember the Frugal Gourmet's perfect advice: "Most seafoods . . . should be simply threatened with heat and then celebrated with joy."

I like to serve this as a first course or as a light supper. If you cannot find pomegranate molasses, you can use a tablespoon of pomegranate juice or even grenadine.

. . . .

1. In a large bowl, combine the shrimp, pomegranate molasses, garlic, turmeric, chile powder, coriander, and salt. Mix well. The best way to do this is with your hands.

2. Heat the vegetable oil in a medium skillet over medium heat. When it shimmers, add the curry leaves and shallots. Cook for 2 to 3 minutes, until the shallots just begin to change color.

3. Add the shrimp and marinade. Toss for a few minutes, just until the shrimp are completely cooked through.

4. Remove from the heat and serve immediately, sprinkled with pomegranate seeds.

Note: Dried pomegranate seeds are not a substitute for fresh ones—trust me on this. Add the dried ones to this recipe and you will have a mess on your hands!

1½ pounds shrimp, shelled and deveined
2 tablespoons pomegranate molasses
1 teaspoon minced garlic
½ teaspoon ground turmeric
¼ teaspoon red chile powder or red chile flakes
½ teaspoon ground coriander
¼ teaspoon table salt
2 tablespoons vegetable oil
1 sprig fresh curry leaves
2 large or 4 to 6 small shallots, thinly sliced
1 cup fresh pomegranate seeds (see Note)

STUFFED BUTTERFISH

SERVES *4*

PREP/COOK TIME:
20 minutes

4 butterfish, cleaned (1 to
1½ pounds total)

4 whole red chiles

1 tablespoon fresh lemon
juice

½ teaspoon ground
turmeric

1 teaspoon table salt

1½-inch piece fresh
ginger, peeled

2 or 3 garlic cloves

2 tablespoons rice flour
such as Mochiko's
Sweet Rice Flour (see
Note)

4 to 5 teaspoons vegetable
oil

Pomfret is very popular in India. The closest fish that I have found here is the butterfish. This simple recipe really brings out the flavor of the fish. While the traditional recipe uses tamarind for tanginess, I use lemon juice, which I always have available. This fish is eaten with the skin, which has a very mild taste. Butterfish are very bony, so eat carefully! Serve with your favorite chutney.

. . . .

1. Using a sharp knife, make several slits through the skin on the butterfish. Set aside.

2. Grind together in a mini food processor or a spice grinder the chiles, lemon juice, turmeric, salt, ginger, and garlic. Rub the paste all over the butterfish, making sure to get it into all the slits and inside the belly cavity.

3. Lightly dredge the butterfish in the rice flour.

4. Heat the oil in a large lidded skillet over medium heat. When the oil begins to shimmer, add the butterfish. Fry for 3 to 4 minutes. Flip over, cover, and cook for another 3 to 4 minutes or until the fish is golden brown on the outside and completely cooked through on the inside.

5. Serve immediately.

Note: Sweet rice flour is made with glutinous rice. You can use regular rice flour as a substitute here.

Tamarind-Glazed Honey Shrimp

*L*ife simply cannot get better than having these shrimp served on a bed of Boston lettuce for lunch or over steamed white rice for dinner. I use the same marinade for chicken as well. Increase the pepper if you like more heat.

. . . .

1. In a large bowl, combine the lemon juice, salt, chile flakes, coriander, chutney, honey, and ginger. Mix well. Add the shrimp and toss well to coat all the shrimp. Cover and refrigerate until almost ready to serve.

2. About 10 minutes before you are ready to serve, heat the vegetable oil in a large skill over medium-high heat. Just before the oil starts smoking, add the shrimp and marinade to the pan. Be careful, as it will splatter.

3. The shrimp will begin to turn a beautiful brick red. Sauté for about 1 minute or until the shrimp are no longer translucent. Transfer to a serving bowl and pour any liquid from the pan over the shrimp. Serve warm.

1 tablespoon fresh lemon juice

¼ teaspoon salt

½ teaspoon red chile flakes (optional)

½ teaspoon coriander seeds, crushed

1 tablespoon store-bought tamarind-date chutney

1 tablespoon liquid honey

1 teaspoon grated peeled fresh ginger

1 pound medium shrimp, peeled and deveined

2 tablespoons vegetable oil

Dry Crab Masala

Serves *4*

Prep/Cook time:

45 minutes

2 tablespoons vegetable oil

1 cinnamon stick

1 teaspoon cumin seeds

½ medium red onion, chopped

1 tablespoon store-bought ginger-garlic paste

2 small green serrano chiles minced

2 small tomatoes, chopped

1 tablespoon ground coriander

1 teaspoon ground turmeric

½ teaspoon red chile powder or red chile flakes

½ cup water

1 pound jumbo lump crab meat such as Phillips brand, picked over

Table salt to taste

Fresh cilantro sprigs for garnish

I use lump crab meat from the grocery store for this easy recipe.

. . . .

1. Heat the oil in a large skillet over medium heat. When the oil begins to shimmer, add the cinnamon stick and cumin. When the whole spices begin to sizzle, add the onion and ginger-garlic paste. Cook for 3 to 5 minutes, until the onion begins to change color.

2. Add the green chiles and tomatoes. Cook for another 12 to 15 minutes, until the tomatoes are soft and oil begins to separate from the mixture. (Use a potato masher to mash the tomatoes to help reduce the cooking time.)

3. Add the coriander, turmeric, and chile powder. Mix well. Add ½ cup water and continue to cook until the water evaporates, 3 to 5 minutes.

4. Add the crab and salt. Cook until the crab is completely heated through, 3 to 5 minutes.

5. Garnish with fresh cilantro and serve hot.

Hot, Hotter, Hottest Shrimp

*f*or this recipe, use the chiles that you love best. This dish is definitely spicy, with the potential to get spicier depending on the chiles that you use.

. . . .

1. In a large bowl, combine the vinegar, lemon zest, chile powder, turmeric, and ½ teaspoon salt. Add the shrimp and mix well. Cover and refrigerate for about 20 minutes.

2. Heat the vegetable oil in a large skillet over high heat. When the oil shimmers, add the onion and green and red chiles and sauté for 3 to 4 minutes, until the onion begins to change color. Add the sugar and cook for another minute. Add the peanuts.

3. Drain the marinade from the shrimp and add the shrimp to the onion mixture. Cook over high heat for 2 to 3 minutes, until the shrimp are completely cooked through. Add salt, if necessary. Serve immediately.

Serves *4*

Prep/Cook Time:
15 minutes hands-on plus 20 minutes refrigeration

½ cup vinegar

½ teaspoon grated lemon zest

1 teaspoon red chile powder or red chile flakes

½ teaspoon ground turmeric

½ teaspoon table salt to start

1 pound jumbo shrimp (26–30 per pound), peeled and deveined

2 tablespoons vegetable oil

½ large red onion, thinly sliced

4 small green serrano chiles, slit lengthwise

2 whole dried red chiles, broken

½ teaspoon sugar

¼ cup chopped dry-roasted peanuts

SALMON WITH KUMQUAT CHUTNEY

SERVES 2

PREP/COOK TIME:

40 minutes, mostly unattended

3 tablespoons Kumquat
and Mango Chutney
with Onion Seeds
(page 41)
1 tablespoon fresh lemon
juice
2 salmon steaks, about 8
ounces each
¼ teaspoon table salt
¼ teaspoon red chile
flakes

*S*almon is one of the most popular choice in our house for dinner. I have tried to devise several ways to prepare it to keep boredom at bay and here is one of my favorites. If you don't have the kumquat chutney, you can use store-bought Major Grey's. I don't like using salt in this recipe. There are such deep flavors with the chutney that, honestly, I don't miss it. I add it here at the insistence of my husband, who would salt his salt, if I let him!

. . . .

1. In a blender, puree the chutney and lemon juice to a thick paste.

2. Preheat the oven to 425°F. Line a baking sheet with foil.

3. Place the salmon steaks on the baking sheet in a single layer. Season them with the salt and chile flakes.

4. Using a spoon, or better, your hands, spread a layer of the paste on the salmon. Flip it over and do the same on the other side.

5. Bake for 30 minutes or until the salmon is cooked through. The paste will form a delicate crust on top of the salmon.

6. Serve immediately.

Fennel-Rubbed Fish Fillets

This is my absolute favorite recipe, and it could not be simpler. Use the fennel-chile rub on page 40. You can either pan-fry or grill the fish and serve it over greens for a light and aromatic salad.

. . . .

1. Lay the fillets on a plate and pat them dry. Sprinkle evenly on both sides with the dry rub. Sprinkle with a little salt to taste.

2. Heat the oil over high heat in a large skillet until hot but not smoking. When the oil begins to shimmer, add the fish. Cook for 3 to 4 minutes on each side, until the fish is crispy on the outside and completely cooked on the inside. Transfer to a paper towel to drain.

3. Serve immediately with your favorite chutney.

If you prefer, you can make a paste of the rub with a little fresh lemon juice and rub it onto the fish.

Serves 4
Prep/Cook time:
15 minutes

4 small white fish fillets such as tilapia, about 1 pound total
1½ tablespoons Fennel-Chile Dry Rub (page 40)
Table salt
3 to 4 tablespoons vegetable oil

PAN-SEARED TROUT WITH MINT-CILANTRO CHUTNEY

SERVES *4*

PREP/COOK TIME:
15 minutes

4 skin-on trout fillets,
about 6 ounces each,
halved lengthwise
Table salt
Freshly ground black
pepper
1 tablespoon vegetable oil
¼ cup Mint-Cilantro
Chutney (page 36)

If you are reading this recipe and thinking, "Really, can it be that simple?"—yes, it is, and it is simply delicious. Don't take my word for it, though. Get a pan out and start searing! Serve the trout with a drizzle of the Mint-Cilantro Chutney (page 36) or a side of the Red Pepper and Green Tomatillo Chutney (page 38).

. . . .

1. Season the trout fillets with salt and pepper.

2. Heat the oil in a large skillet over medium heat. When the oil begins to shimmer, add the trout, skin side down. Cook for 2 to 3 minutes. Flip over and cook for another 3 to 4 minutes, until the trout is cooked through.

3. Transfer to a plate lined with paper towels, skin side down.

4. Place each fillet on a serving plate and drizzle each with up to a tablespoon of chutney. Serve immediately.

MONICA'S TOMATO AND COCONUT FISH CURRY

Everyone has a signature dish, something that they are really proud of—and this one is mine. I have been cooking it for as long as I can remember. It is a favorite with adults and kids alike. My dad once told me it was *his* favorite. I cannot tell you how happy I was, since he has such discerning tastes. He made it for me once, and it was quite interesting. "I won't add the mustard seeds, since I don't like mustard. I don't have any curry leaves so they won't go in either. I will sauté some onions first, and then add tomatoes and I prefer ground coriander, so I will add that. But you know, I do add the coconut milk, so it is just like yours!"

. . . .

1. In a large skillet, heat the oil over medium heat. When the oil begins to shimmer, add the mustard seeds. As soon as they crackle, add the curry leaves, ginger, garlic, and green chile. Sauté for a few seconds to combine.

2. Add the tomato. Cook gently for 10 to 12 minutes, until the tomato is soft and the oil begins to leave the side of the mixture. You can add some water if the tomato begins to stick. I sometimes add a quarter-cup of water and cover the pan for 5 to 6 minutes. This helps cook the tomatoes faster. Then I uncover it and continue to cook until all the water evaporates.

3. Stir in the turmeric, chile powder, and salt. Cook for 1 minute.

4. Stir in the fish and cook for 5 minutes.

5. Add the coconut milk. Let the mixture come to a boil, then lower the heat and simmer, stirring occasionally, until the fish is tender. Serve immediately.

SERVES *4*

PREP/COOK TIME:

40 minutes

2 tablespoons vegetable oil

1 teaspoon black mustard seeds

10 fresh curry leaves

1-inch piece peeled fresh ginger, grated

3 garlic cloves, crushed

1 small green serrano chile, chopped

1 large tomato, chopped

1 teaspoon turmeric

1 teaspoon red chile powder

¼ teaspoon table salt to start

1 pound catfish fillets, cut into bite-sized pieces

½ of a 13.5-ounce can coconut milk (¾ cup plus 2 tablespoons)

CRABBY VERMICELLI

Serves 6 to 8

Prep/Cook time:

30 minutes

4 tablespoons vegetable
  oil, divided
One 7-ounce package
  Indian short-cut
  vermicelli such as
  Bambino brand, about
  2 cups
1 teaspoon black mustard
  seeds
1 teaspoon cumin seeds
Pinch of asafetida
2 whole dried red chiles,
  crushed
1 cup frozen vegetable
  mix (carrots and peas
  are good), thawed
1 cup hot water and
  additional water as
  indicated on the
  vermicelli package
1 cup lump crabmeat such
  as Phillips brand,
  picked over
Table salt
Fresh basil leaves for
  garnish

Most Indian vermicelli dishes are vegetarian but I like this with crab. You can also make it with leftover cooked chicken. With its mild flavor, this is a perfect dish for kids to enjoy. You can add some dry-roasted peanuts at the end if you like.

The trick to getting this dish to taste right is using the right volume of water. The directions on packages of vermicelli vary slightly from brand to brand. Follow the package directions for best results.

. . . .

1. Heat 2 tablespoons of the oil in a deep skillet over medium heat. Add the vermicelli and toast for 3 to 4 minutes, until it just begins to turn golden brown. Stir constantly or the vermicelli will burn. Transfer the vermicelli to a plate or bowl and set aside.

2. Return the skillet to medium heat and add the remaining 2 tablespoons oil. When the oil shimmers, add the mustard seeds, cumin seeds, asafetida, and the chiles.

3. As soon as the mustard seeds begin to sizzle, about 1 minute or so, add the vegetables. Sauté them for 3 to 4 minutes. Add 1 cup hot water and continue to cook on medium heat until all the water evaporates and the vegetables are cooked.

4. Add the crab and salt to taste and mix well. Cook, stirring, until the vegetables and the crab are well coated with the spice mixture, about another minute.

5. Add the water called for on the vermicelli package, increase the heat to high, and bring to a boil.

6. Reduce the heat to medium. Add the vermicelli. Cook uncovered until the water is absorbed, about 10 minutes. Stir occasionally.

7. Serve hot, garnished with fresh basil.

TILAPIA CURRY
WITH ROASTED SPICES

SERVES *4 to 6*

PREP/COOK TIME:

30 minutes

2 whole dried red chiles

2 teaspoons coriander
seeds

1 teaspoon cumin seeds

½ teaspoon peppercorns

½ teaspoon fenugreek
seeds

2 tablespoons vegetable
oil

1 medium red onion,
minced

2 teaspoons minced
peeled fresh ginger

2 teaspoons minced garlic

1 teaspoon ground
turmeric

¼ teaspoon table salt

One 13.5-ounce can
coconut milk (see
Note)

1 pound tilapia fillets,
cubed

Tilapia takes really well to spices. You can prepare this
curry a day in advance, which will give the spices a chance
to bring out their true flavors. I like to serve this with steamed
rice. If you like thicker curries, reduce the coconut milk by half.

. . . .

1. Heat a small dry skillet over medium heat. Add the chiles,
coriander, cumin, peppercorns, and fenugreek and roast for 30 to
45 seconds, until the spices are fragrant. Remove from the heat
immediately. Allow to cool down then grind to a fine powder in
a spice grinder.

2. Heat the vegetable oil in a large deep skillet over medium
heat. Add the onion, ginger, and garlic and cook for 4 to 5 minutes, until the onion changes color to a light brown.

3. Add the turmeric, the roasted ground spices, and salt and stir
to combine.

4. Add the coconut milk and bring to a gentle boil.

5. Add the tilapia and cook over medium-low heat until the fish
is cooked through, about 10 minutes.

6. Serve hot with steamed rice.

$\mathcal{N}$ote: Using canned coconut milk for sauces sounds simple enough and yet there is a small trick to it. If you are using the regular milk (not the "lite" one), when you open the can, you will notice that the coconut cream has risen to the top of the can. Use a spoon to mix this with all the liquid at the bottom of the can and then use the coconut milk. Usually, lite coconut milk will not have the same issue. You can store unused coconut milk, covered, in the refrigerator for up to a week.

CATFISH TAMARIND CURRY

SERVES *4*

PREP/COOK TIME:

35 minutes

1 cup fresh cilantro leaves,
  lightly packed

4 small green serrano
  chiles (or less if you
  don't want the heat)

1-inch piece fresh ginger,
  peeled and coarsely
  chopped

2 garlic cloves, peeled

2 tablespoons store-
  bought tamarind-date
  chutney

2 tablespoons vegetable
  oil

1 teaspoon ground
  turmeric

¼ teaspoon table salt to
  start

One 13.5-ounce can
  coconut milk

1 pound catfish fillets,
  cubed

*Y*ou can use any mild, white-fleshed fish for this very spicy recipe that really packs a punch. Stronger fish like salmon will not do this curry justice. Shrimp works well here, too. If you don't have the tamarind chutney, you can add a tablespoon of fresh lemon juice. The curry of this dish is thin—it is meant to be eaten with steamed rice. If you like thicker curries, reduce the coconut milk by half.

. . . .

1. In a food processor, grind the cilantro, chiles, ginger, garlic, and tamarind chutney to a paste. You can use a couple of table-spoons of warm water to aid in the process.

2. Heat the vegetable oil in a medium skillet over high heat. When the oil shimmers, add the spice paste and reduce the heat to medium. Add the turmeric and salt and allow the paste to come to a gentle boil.

3. Add the coconut milk and cook for another 5 minutes, bring-ing the curry to another gentle boil. Cook for 5 to 6 minutes, until the curry just begins to thicken.

4. Add the fish. Cook for about 10 minutes, until the fish is cooked through.

5. Serve hot with steamed rice.

SAFFRON MUSSEL STEW

This is a super simple dish to make, perfect for a fall evening when the weather is getting cold and you feel like something warm and spicy to comfort and soothe you. Buy a nice loaf of crusty bread to mop up this curry.

. . . .

1. In a deep saucepan, heat the oil over high heat. When the oil shimmers, add the onion, ginger, garlic, curry leaves, and green chiles. Sauté for 4 to 6 minutes, until the onion begins to change color.

2. Add the turmeric and coriander. Mix well and sauté for another 30 seconds.

3. Add the broth and bring to a boil. Reduce the heat to a simmer and add the cream. Remove from the heat and allow to cool to room temperature.

4. Transfer to a blender and blend to a smooth consistency. If you like an even smoother texture, pass the mixture through a sieve. I prefer not to do so.

5. Return the sauce to the saucepan and bring to another gentle boil.

6. Add the mussels and cook, covered, for about 10 minutes, shaking the saucepan occasionally.

7. Add salt to taste and the saffron threads and mix well. Serve hot.

Note: If using whole fresh mussels, you will need 1½ pounds. Soak in cold water for an hour. Discard any that open up. Remove beards and rinse well. Then pat dry and proceed with the recipe.

SERVES 4

PREP/COOK TIME:
25 minutes (longer if using fresh mussels)

2 tablespoons vegetable oil

1 medium red onion, finely chopped

½-inch piece fresh ginger, peeled and finely chopped

3 or 4 garlic cloves, finely chopped

20 fresh curry leaves

2 or 3 small green serrano chiles, finely chopped

½ teaspoon ground turmeric

2 teaspoons ground coriander powder

1½ cups chicken broth

¼ cup heavy cream

1 pound mussels on the half-shell, such as New Zealand Greenshell Mussels

Table salt

A few strands of saffron

SHRIMP IN GREEN-MANGO BUTTER SAUCE

SERVES *4*

COOK TIME: *20 minutes*

3½ tablespoons unsalted
butter

½ teaspoon vegetable oil

1 teaspoon black mustard
seeds

10 fresh curry leaves

2 large or 4 to 6 small
organic shallots, thinly
sliced

2 garlic cloves, thinly
sliced

½ teaspoon ground
turmeric

¼ teaspoon table salt to
start

½ teaspoon coarsely
ground black pepper

¼ cup chicken broth

1½ pounds jumbo shrimp,
peeled and deveined

1 cup diced peeled green
(unripe) mango

1 teaspoon sugar

½ cup water

Half a fresh lemon

Green mangoes cooked in a sweet butter sauce add a delightfully different tart, tangy, and sweet touch to this shrimp curry. Serve this with steamed basmati rice.

. . . .

1. Heat 2½ tablespoons of the butter and the oil in a heavy-bottomed saucepan until the foam subsides. Add the mustard seeds and curry leaves and sauté just until the mustard seeds pop.

2. Add the shallots and garlic and sauté until aromatic and golden, 2 to 3 minutes.

3. Add the turmeric, salt, pepper, broth, and shrimp and simmer a few minutes, until the shrimp are almost cooked through. Remove from the heat.

4. In a medium skillet, melt the remaining 1 tablespoon butter over medium heat. Add the mango and sugar and sauté for 1 minute. Add the water and bring to a boil. Cook for 5 to 7 minutes, until the mango starts to soften.

5. Transfer the mango mixture to the saucepan containing the shrimp. Mix well, then reheat gently.

6. Serve hot with a squeeze of fresh lemon juice.

RICE and BREADS

. . . .

Since I have already given you a good introduction to the diversity of Indian cuisine, I won't repeat myself here. Instead, let me talk to you about the diversity of rice, bread, and rice-breads that you'll find in this chapter.

Let's start with rice. While Indian cooking uses many types of rice, the most popular by far is the very aromatic and nutty basmati rice. It cooks up fast and really does not require much preparation. The beauty of this rice is that it has flavor that can stand alone but it also shines when dressed up with whole spices like cardamom cloves, and becomes the womb for many ingredients like meats, vegetables, and nuts. It works well with both savory and sweet dishes. What I really love about rice in Indian cooking is the transformation that occurs such that the final dish hardly resembles the starting ingredients. For example, one of the most famous dishes of South India is fermented, steamed *idlis*. These small round cakes are made by soaking and then steaming rice and lentils. The same batter used to make idlis can also produce savory pancakes and thin crepes. Rice can also be dried, beaten to a pulp, spiced up, and served for breakfast. So are these rice dishes, breads, or rice-breads? I just call them scrumptious!

Even when rice is just rice, to many it isn't! The first day my son went to school, I decided to be the good mom and pack him a lunch. Rice, I decided, would be the safest option. So I packed him a perfect rice pilaf with cumin, turmeric, and baby peas. He came home crying. "Everyone wanted to know if my rice had gone bad and why it had turned yellow. Why did you give me this, mama, why?" Yes, I now pack him white rice—but it still has peas!

Brown basmati rice is now readily available and it is just as flavorful as the white variety.

As for bread, there are as many types of breads in India as there are pastas in Italy. Breads are made from whole-wheat flour, corn flour, rice flour, and chickpea flour, to mention a few, and can be cooked on the griddle, in the oven, and even in steamers. Breads are flavored with spices and herbs. They may be stuffed or topped with meats, vegetables, lentils, lentil wafers, eggs, or nuts. You name it, and it can be in or on the bread.

I had the pleasure of eating some curry leaf bread in Bangalore. It was heavenly! In Mumbai and other western Indian cities, a bread called *pau*, similar to the traditional American dinner roll, brought to India by the Portuguese, is now very popular as a street food when served with sumptuous vegetables.

So widespread is the taste for Indian breads that Hot Breads, a chain restaurant on the east cost of the United States, sells pau and other Indian favorites stuffed with paneer, chicken, other ground meats, or with the ever-popular potatoes.

So with that brief introduction to breads and rice, I would like to invite you to try some fun versions of traditional Indian favorites. I hope you will enjoy this eclectic collection of recipes.

Please note: the cooking time for rice varies greatly. For all my recipes, I use the largest burner on my gas stove. This gives me perfect rice each time. If you have a less powerful stove, it may take up to 50 percent longer to properly cook rice.

Brown Basmati Rice with Pine Nuts, Mint, and Pomegranate

There are as many ways to make rice as there are birds in the sky, but this is an especially tasty preparation. If you wish to vary this dish, don't add too many other whole spices. Instead vary the nuts, add dried fruits, or choose other herbs. Too many spices will overwhelm the taste of the dish.

Some people like to soak their rice in water for about a half hour. This reduces the cooking time. I generally don't soak my rice.

* * * * * * * * * * * * * * *

1. Rinse the rice well in running water. Drain and set aside.

2. In a deep lidded saucepan, heat the clarified butter over medium heat. Add the bay leaves and cardamom pods. Sauté for 1 minute or until fragrant.

3. Add the salt, lemon juice, and rice. Mix well. Add the water and bring to a rolling boil. Reduce the heat to low. Cover and cook for 18 to 20 minutes, until most of the water has been absorbed. You will see small craters forming on top of the rice.

4. Remove from the heat and let sit, covered, for about 5 minutes.

5. Fluff with a fork, top with the pine nuts, mint leaves, and pomegranate seeds and serve immediately.

Note: To toast pine nuts: Heat a small dry skillet over medium heat. Add the pine nuts and toss gently for about 30 seconds, until they begin to brown. Remove immediately.

Serves 4

Prep/Cook time: 40 minutes, mostly unattended

1 cup brown basmati rice
1 tablespoon clarified butter or ghee (page 22) or vegetable oil
2 bay leaves
2 green cardamom pods, lightly crushed
¼ teaspoon table salt to start
1 teaspoon fresh lemon juice
2 cups water
½ cup toasted pine nuts (see Note)
8 to 10 whole mint leaves
½ cup fresh pomegranate seeds

ONION BREAD STIR-FRY

SERVES *4 to 6*

PREP/COOK TIME:

12 minutes

4 onion-topped dinner
   rolls (about ¾ pound)

2 tablespoons vegetable
   oil (see Note)

1 teaspoon black mustard
   seeds

2 dried whole red chiles

¼ medium red onion,
   minced

⅛ teaspoon table salt

½ teaspoon ground
   turmeric

1 teaspoon sugar

1 tablespoon fresh lemon
   juice

¼ cup salted roasted
   cashews

2 tablespoons minced
   cilantro

was first introduced to this stir-fry when I got married. It is a typical dish of western India, where it is served for breakfast or as a savory snack. My mother-in-law would make it with leftover bread or with leftover *rotis* (Indian griddle bread). When she began to visit us in the United States, she experimented with the wide variety of bread and dinner rolls available here. She found that the onion-topped dinner rolls worked really well for this recipe. She likes to add boiled potatoes to her recipe (right after adding the onions) and also garnishes it with diced fresh tomatoes. I prefer this plainer version to serve with tea.

. . . .

1. Tear the rolls into small pieces and set aside.

2. Heat the oil in a medium skillet on medium heat. When the oil begins to shimmer, add the mustard seeds and chiles. When the mustard seeds crackle, add the onion, salt, turmeric, and sugar. Sauté until the onions are transparent, 2 to 3 minutes.

3. Add the bread to the skillet. Increase the heat. Mix well and cook for another 2 to 3 minutes, until the bread begins to just crisp up.

4. Remove from the heat. Add the lemon juice and cashews and toss well.

5. Serve garnished with minced cilantro.

Note: Bread, obviously, tends to absorb a lot of oil. To ensure that does not happen, or at least to keep it to a minimum, increase the heat when you add the bread and sauté, stirring constantly, to help the bread crisp up quickly.

Brown Rice Pulao with Vegetables and Cumin

Brown basmati rice is very fragrant and works really well with spices. My mother used to make this with white rice but with today's focus on health and nutrition, I adapted the recipe for brown rice. It works perfectly.

. . . .

1. In a deep lidded saucepan, heat the vegetable oil over medium heat. When the oil shimmers, add the cumin seeds. As soon as the seeds begin to sizzle, add the onion and garlic. Sauté for 4 to 5 minutes, until the onion changes color and softens.

2. Add the tomato and cook for about 5 minutes or until the tomato is soft. Add the vegetables and cook for another 6 to 7 minutes.

3. Reduce the heat to medium. Add the turmeric, chile powder, and coriander and mix well. Add the rice and salt and mix well. Add the water and bring to a rolling boil. Reduce the heat to low, cover, and cook until all the water has been absorbed. This should take 15 to 20 minutes.

4. When the rice is cooked, fluff it with a fork and transfer it to a platter. Top with the cilantro and serve immediately.

Did you know . . . brown basmati rice cooks the same way as regular basmati rice, 1 cup rice to 2 cups water. Combine the rice and water in a pot and bring to a boil. Lower the heat to a simmer, cover, and cook for about 20 minutes or until all the water has been absorbed.

SERVE *4 to 6*

PREP/COOK TIME:

40 minutes

2 tablespoons vegetable oil

1 teaspoon cumin seeds

½ small red onion, thinly sliced

1 garlic clove, minced

1 small tomato, diced

1 cup frozen vegetables (peas, corn, or mixed)

½ teaspoon ground turmeric

½ teaspoon red chile powder or red chile flakes

1 teaspoon crushed coriander seeds

1 cup brown basmati rice

¼ teaspoon table salt

2 cups water

Fresh cilantro sprigs for garnish

MAKES *6 large pancakes or*
12 tiny pancakes

PREP/COOK TIME:
30 minutes

2 cups uncooked Cream
of Wheat (I use the
2½-minute enriched
Cream of Wheat)
1 cup plain yogurt
1 teaspoon table salt
1 cup water
½ cup finely grated
paneer
½ cup finely diced oven-
roasted tomatoes such
as Divina, or regular
canned diced tomatoes,
drained well
2 small green serrano
chiles, minced
2 to 3 tablespoons minced
cilantro

CREAM OF WHEAT
AND PANEER PANCAKES
WITH OVEN-ROASTED TOMATOES

This is one of those rice-bread dishes. Traditionally the dish uses a rice and lentil batter that is left to ferment overnight (or several nights, depending on how cold the weather gets); the resulting batter is steamed. While it tastes delicious prepared this way, it is a very time-consuming method. I use a modified Cream of Wheat batter. (Some Indian grocers are starting to carry prepared batter, so if you can find a batter labeled *Idli* or *Dosa* batter, you can use that in this recipe.)

You can really play with the additions: try red bell peppers, cooked corn kernels, or different types of chiles.

. . . .

1. In a large bowl, combine the Cream of Wheat, yogurt, salt, and water to make a lump-free, thick but pourable batter.

2. Add the paneer, tomatoes, chiles, cilantro, onion, cumin seeds, and pepper to taste and mix well. Add another 2 tablespoons water if the batter appears too thick.

3. Heat a medium nonstick skillet over medium heat.

4. Add 1 tablespoon of the vegetable oil and when the oil is hot, add a generous ½ cup of the batter. (For smaller pancakes, use ¼ cup.)

5. Swirl the pan to spread the batter into a circle about 6 inches in diameter.

6. When the batter bubbles on top and the edges begin to brown, 2½ to 3 minutes, flip over.

7. Cook another 2½ to 3 minutes, until the batter has totally set. The outside should be brown and crisp and the inside should be completely cooked (no liquid batter).

8. Transfer the pancake to a warm serving platter. Repeat until you have used up all the batter. Keep warm in a low oven.

9. Serve immediately with Mint-Cilantro Chutney.

¼ small red onion finely diced
1 teaspoon cumin seeds
Freshly ground black pepper
6 tablespoons vegetable oil
Mint-Cilantro Chutney (page 36)

PANEER AND FIG PIZZA

SERVES *4*

PREP/COOK TIME: *20 minutes*

One 12-inch packaged
    pizza crust or use a
    crust from homemade
    pizza dough
Nonstick cooking spray
1 cup crumbled or grated
    paneer
1 cup ricotta cheese
8 to 10 very ripe figs,
    trimmed and thinly
    sliced
Table salt
⅛ teaspoon ground white
    pepper
8 to 10 basil leaves

One of the best-selling items on the menu at Domino's in Delhi is the pizza topped with chicken tikka. Yes, Indians do love pizza, and it is very much a part of the modern Indian food scene. But it is nothing new. My mother has made "pizza" since I was about five years old. She used a simple homemade dough topped with a homemade tomato sauce and my choice of chicken or vegetables. It was not called pizza, of course. I called it chicken *wali roti* (a chicken bread). When my son was younger, I took him to an eatery/children's play area in Delhi called Eatopia. It serves a very popular version of Indian pizza called a *Naanza*, a naan dough topped with tandoori chicken or a variety of vegetarian toppings. We both fell in love with it. And it really is the same concept as a regular pizza—great dough with the choicest of toppings. Incidentally, Zante's in San Francisco has sold Indian pizza since 1993. And California Pizza Kitchen serves a mango–tandoori chicken pizza. I could go on and on.

I call this a gentle pizza; the flavors are mild, yet so satisfying. This dish is sweet thanks to the figs—which are, I think, the world's sweetest fruit. While paneer gives this dish a unique taste, it is not a melting cheese. I have added some ricotta to make the topping a bit creamier.

This dish depends on only one thing—the ripeness of the fresh figs. If the figs are not sweet, the dish will not taste good no matter what you do. Alternatively, I have made it with dried figs from Nutra Figs (which I love) and it is pretty good—if you cannot find fresh figs, that is. Incidentally, there are many varieties of dried figs that really make the fig taste like cardboard. Nutra figs are actually still moist and really, really sweet.

. . . .

1. Preheat the oven to 350°F. Spray the crust with a mist of non-stick cooking spay.

2. In a bowl, combine the paneer and ricotta and mix well. Spread the cheese mixture evenly over the crust. Top with the figs, and sprinkle with salt and pepper.

3. Bake according to the directions given with the crust, usually about 10 to 12 minutes. The cheese will brown a little but it is not a melting cheese so don't expect it to bubble.

4. Serve topped with fresh basil leaves. If your figs are really ripe, this will taste like a dessert!

For a savory version, combine the paneer with some minced cilantro, diced red onions, and diced bell peppers.

WILD MUSHROOM AND PANEER PILAF

Serves 4

Prep/Cook time:

35 minutes, mostly unattended

3 tablespoons vegetable
  oil
½ small red onion, sliced
  thinly
1 garlic clove, minced
3 cups chopped fresh
  mushrooms such as
  oyster, cremini, or
  button
½ teaspoon ground
  turmeric
½ teaspoon red chile
  powder or red chile
  flakes
1 teaspoon crushed
  coriander seeds
2 teaspoons dried
  fenugreek leaves
1 cup white basmati rice
¼ teaspoon table salt
2 cups water
1 cup paneer cut into bite-
  sized cubes
Fresh cilantro sprigs for
  garnish

Basmati rice perfectly complements sautéed paneer and wild mushrooms in this recipe. You can serve this on its own or combine it with a cup of whipped yogurt mixed with a hint of garlic, freshly cracked pepper, and fresh cilantro.

. . . .

1. In a deep lidded saucepan, heat 2 tablespoons of the vegetable oil over medium heat. When the oil shimmers, add the onion and garlic. Sauté for 4 to 5 minutes, until the onion changes color and softens.

2. Add the mushrooms and sauté over medium-high heat until the mushrooms begin to brown. This will take about 5 minutes. The mushrooms will release some moisture; continue cooking until the water they release evaporates.

3. Reduce the heat to medium. Add the turmeric, chile powder, coriander, and fenugreek and mix well. Add the rice and salt and mix well. Add the water and bring to a rolling boil. Reduce the heat to low, cover, and cook until all the water has been absorbed. This should take 12 to 15 minutes.

4. While the rice is cooking, prepare the paneer. Heat the remaining 1 tablespoon oil in a medium skillet over medium heat. When the oil shimmers, add the paneer cubes. Fry, stirring, for a few minutes, until the paneer is lightly golden. Remove with a slotted spoon and place on a paper towel to drain.

5. Fluff the rice with a fork and transfer to a warmed platter. Top with the paneer and cilantro and serve immediately.

Did you know . . . shiitake mushrooms have about double the calories and three to four times as much carbohydrates as other mushrooms.

Serves 4

Prep/Cook time:
*20 minutes, including time to
make the omelet*

1½ cups frozen mixed
  vegetables, such as
  peas/corn/green beans

2 tablespoons vegetable
  oil

1-inch piece fresh ginger,
  peeled and cut into fine
  matchsticks

2 garlic cloves, sliced

2 whole cloves

1 cinnamon stick

1 black cardamom pod

¼ cup soy sauce

1 tablespoon vinegar

½ teaspoon red chile
  flakes

2 scallions, white and pale
  green parts only, finely
  chopped

1 cup cooked boneless
  chicken cut into ½-inch
  dice

Of Rice and Zen

Chinese influence on Indian cooking is apparent in popular Indian restaurants in India and now even here in the United States (we have a Masala Wok in Virginia!). This is an Indian-Chinese recipe, and is, once again, not some new "fusion" idea that I created. The intriguing combination of Indian ingredients such as garam masala (warm spice mix), cilantro, and tamarind in combination with Chinese soy sauce, ginger, garlic, and even ketchup comes from a cuisine that has been in India for years. Chinese immigrants settled on the eastern coast of India decades ago, and this cuisine is a culmination of two very different food cultures coming together. Almost any menu in an everyday eatery in Delhi and Mumbai will list several Indian-Chinese dishes. On our family trips to Mumbai, the first meal we eat out is not traditional Indian, but Indian-Chinese!

Please note: This recipe uses previously cooked plain basmati rice, which really does need to be cold for this stir-fry. So if you want to make this dish, make the rice the day before and let it sit in the refrigerator for the night.

. . . .

1. Cook the frozen vegetables in the microwave according to directions on the package. Drain and set aside when done.

2. In a large nonstick skillet, heat the vegetable oil over high heat. When the oil shimmers, add the ginger, garlic, cloves, cinnamon stick, cardamom, and mixed vegetables. Sauté for about 1 minute.

3. Add the soy sauce, vinegar, and chile flakes and mix well. Add the scallions and chicken and sauté for another 2 minutes or until the chicken is completely heated through.

4. Add the cold rice and mix well. Sauté for 2 to 3 minutes, until the rice is completely heated through.

5. Serve hot, topped with the egg strips and cilantro.

3 cups cooked white rice, preferably basmati, refrigerated

One 1-egg omelet, cut into thin strips

1 tablespoon chopped fresh cilantro

SHRIMP RICE

SERVES 4

PREP/COOK TIME:
40 minutes

3 tablespoons vegetable
   oil
1 small red onion, roughly
   chopped
1-inch piece fresh ginger,
   peeled and cut into fine
   matchsticks
1 medium tomato,
   chopped
1 small green serrano
   chile, chopped
1 teaspoon ground
   turmeric
½ teaspoon red chile
   powder or red chile
   flakes
1 tablespoon coriander
   seeds, crushed
1 teaspoon ground cumin
1 pound medium shrimp,
   peeled and deveined

Remember Bubba, who lectured his friend Forrest Gump about the many wonders of shrimp, America's most beloved seafood? Americans eat more shrimp than any other seafood, according to a report released by the American Seafood Distributors Association in June 2004. Bubba said:

Shrimp is the fruit of the sea. You can barbecue it, boil it, broil it, bake it, sauté it . . . Pan-fried, deep-fried, stir-fried. There's pineapple shrimp, lemon shrimp, coconut shrimp, pepper shrimp, shrimp soup, shrimp stew, shrimp salad, shrimp and potatoes, shrimp burger, shrimp sandwich. That—that's about it.

Bubba was wrong; he short-changed this fabulous creature with respect to its endless possibilities. It can also be combined with coriander, cilantro, cumin, garlic, ginger, or green chiles to provide a range of flavors from salty to sweet to sour to spicy—to all of them together. Here is one of my favorite shrimp dishes that marries the shrimp to the heat of the spices and the gentleness of white rice.

. . . .

1. In a deep lidded saucepan, heat the vegetable oil over medium heat. Add the onion and sauté for 5 to 7 minutes, until soft.

2. Add the ginger and cook for another minute.

3. Add the tomato and mix well. Cook, stirring, for about 10 minutes, until the tomato is completely cooked and the oil separates from the onion-tomato mixture. To aid in this process, you can add a few tablespoons of water especially if the mixture begins to dry up and stick to the sides of the pan.

4. Add the green chile, turmeric, chile powder, coriander, and cumin and mix well. Cook for another minute, then add the shrimp. Mix well. Add the rice, salt, and water. Stir well to mix all the ingredients.

5. Bring to a rolling boil then reduce the heat to low. Cover and cook for 12 to 15 minutes, until most of the water has been absorbed. You will see small craters forming on top of the rice.

6. Remove from the heat and let sit, covered, for about 5 minutes. Fluff with a fork as the shrimp will have settled at the bottom. Garnish with minced cilantro. Serve hot.

Note: If your rice cooks too firm, you used too little water; if it cooks too mushy, you used too much water. If you are unsure of how much water to use, start with 1 cup rice to 2 cups water as a guideline. If you soak your rice prior to use, reduce the water to 1¾ cups for 1 cup of rice.

1 cup white basmati rice, well rinsed and drained
¼ teaspoon table salt
2 cups water
Minced fresh cilantro for garnish

Veiled Treasures

"Be careful with that," Chef Qureshi directs the server. "Be gentle, serve it *gently*." The nervous young server carefully removes the pastry *purdah* (veil) from the *biryani* and, using a small silver serving spoon and very shaky hands, scoops up some rice and places it on my plate. He then goes back to the dish and finds a morel stuffed with pomegranate seeds and grated cheese and places it on top of my rice, as the chef looks on intently. A spoonful of garlic-infused yogurt is added to the side. "Stop," the chef waves his hands emphatically, almost giving the young server a nervous heart attack, "no more. We need to savor this bite by bite."

We are seated in the grand coffee shop of the ITC's Grand Maratha Hotel in Mumbai. I am in the company of Grand Master Indian Chef Imtiaz Qureshi, who has been with the ITC group of hotels since 1976 and who has played host to celebrities and politicians from India's Nehru to America's Clinton. This charming old chef is what legends are made of; he has graced the cover of *Newsweek* in India and is credited with reviving a very ancient Indian cuisine *dum phukt*, or cooking with steam.

I am a biryani lover and by a stroke of luck was given the liberty to ask for a dream—to have the chef personally cook his signature biryani for me. I spent my dream date watching this dynamo, aged seventy-five, in his kitchen preparing this dish. His movements clearly indicated the kitchen was his life and his demeanor proved he was and always will be the king of the kitchen. The junior kitchen staff scurried to honor each request, clearly in awe of this man. As he began to prepare the biryani, a gentle aroma filled the kitchen.

He makes it look so easy, I thought. I guess if I had cooked the dish repeatedly for fifty odd years, I could have had the same practiced and easy stance as he did! He was meticulous in his preparation, clearly looking upset if any small thing was out of proportion. "It's all about the small things," he told me repeatedly, "all about the details."

Biryani, an Indian rice dish cooked with vegetables, meats, dried fruit and many aromatic spices, has always had lovers or haters. There never seem to be in-betweens. This dish owes its roots to Persia. In fact, the word itself originates from the Persian word *birian* which means fried before cooking. Through history's turns and twists, the dish found a home in Indian kitchens hundreds of years ago. "Biryanis are prepared traditionally with meats that are fried and then cooked with rice," he tells me. "India boasts over twenty types of biryanis. The cooking methods, ingredients, and even the rice used are different in each. Even the proportions of rice and meat vary in the dish." Aroma is a big part of the biryani from Lucknow, the birthplace of this accomplished chef. The use of aged basmati rice to prepare the biryani, claims Chef Qureshi, doubles the aroma of the dish. From brown rice biryani, to biryani prepared over hot coals, to biryani prepared in a coconut shell, the combinations are endless and always delicious.

I follow him around the kitchen with a pen in my hand taking down each word he utters about the biryani. I don't have to ask a single question; he begins to talk about his love for biryani and there is no stopping him. The chef speaks in pure Urdu, a language I am familiar with but by no means an expert in. Noticing my occasional blank looks he stops to explain in simpler terms. Although he cannot read or write, his ideas, thoughts, and philosophies about food are like poetry. The conversation feels like a walk on a winding, forested path—offering twists as he recalls funny incidents and cool shade as he reminisces about the loving people in his life. A former wrestler, he has cooked as long as he can remember, he tells me. "Come here," he says and places a morel in my hand, "feel that, now we can stuff it. Always feel the food you are cooking with."

I lead him into talking about the dish he allowed me to watch him prepare—his morel biryani. Fifty years ago Chef Qureshi first saw morels in India. His mother thought they looked like a cow's stomach, he jokes. He saw them used in a mushroom pilaf (a simpler version of a biryani, he tells me—often pilafs won't be spiced as a biryani is). He liked it and used it at ITC to eventually create a biryani that is unique and not found in commonplace Indian cookbooks. The side dish to this Lucknowi biryani is known as a *boorani*, or a dish with a strong smell. It is a yogurt dish laced with garlic. The chef tells me it is served along with the biryani as it aids in *hazmaa* or the digestion of the biryani.

Later that afternoon, I am seated with him at a table in the coffee shop, about to taste his signature dish. He stares at me anxiously, waiting for me to take my first bite. With shaking hands, I pick up my fork and take my first bite. His intense scrutiny intensifies as he watches each expression on my face. Tangy pomegranate, mild cheese, and velvety mushroom charm my palette as the earthy fragrance from the rice entices my sense of smell. I smile, and the chef leans back. "This is the way to eat a biryani, slowly, and relishing each bite," he declares.

I attempt to continue the interview. "A ready biryani is like a beautiful lady," Chef Qureshi says with a twinkle in his eye. "They both must never be kept waiting. The interview is over, now you eat." ❋

SPICED BEATEN RICE

$\mathcal{H}$ere is a great traditional dish of *poha* (beaten rice). I don't mess with it much since it is already so simple and easy to make. You can add nuts or potatoes and carrots if you wish.

. . . .

1. Place the poha in a large bowl. Add the milk slowly, making sure it moistens all the poha. Set aside.

2. In a deep skillet, heat the oil over medium heat. When it begins to shimmer, add the mustard seeds. When the seeds begin to sputter, add the curry leaves, green chiles, turmeric, chile powder, and salt. Mix well.

3. Add the onion and sauté for about 2 to 3 minutes, until the onion begins to change color and soften.

4. Add the peas and mix well. Add the poha and mix well. Add the water.

5. Increase the heat to high. Continue to cook, stirring constantly, until the poha has mixed totally with the other ingredients and is completely cooked through. This will take 3 to 4 minutes. The water should be almost completely absorbed. The poha's texture will change to become soft and it will look like rice when it is cooked.

6. Add the peanuts and mix well.

7. Remove from the heat. Garnish with cilantro and a sprinkle of lemon juice. Allow to sit for about 10 minutes to give the flavors a chance to meld. Serve.

$\mathcal{D}$id you know . . . *poha* (beaten rice) is rice which has been flattened into flakes. Stores sell a thin or thick variety. It is reconstituted using water or milk. It is used to make snacks and other dishes and is a very popular breakfast treat.

SERVES *4*
PREP/COOK TIME: *20 minutes*

2 cups thick poha

1 cup whole milk

2 tablespoons vegetable oil

1 teaspoon black mustard seeds

10 curry leaves

2 small green serrano chiles, slit lengthwise

½ teaspoon ground turmeric

½ to 1 teaspoon red chile powder or red chile flakes (to taste)

¼ teaspoon table salt

½ small red onion, sliced

1 cup cooked green peas

1 cup water

¼ cup whole dry-roasted peanuts

Fresh cilantro leaves for garnish

1 tablespoon fresh lemon juice

MOREL PULAO WITH CASHEWS

SERVES *4 to 6*

PREP/COOK TIME:
*45 minutes, plus 30 minutes
soaking*

12 to 15 large dried
   morels
½ cup raw cashews
2 cups hot water
¼ cup grated paneer
2 teaspoons finely
   chopped fresh mint
   leaves
⅛ plus ½ teaspoon table
   salt
¼ cup vegetable oil
1 green cardamom pod
1 bay leaf
1 cinnamon stick
1 small red onion, pureed
Table salt
½ teaspoon red chile
   flakes
2¾ cups chicken stock
1 cup white basmati rice,
   rinsed and drained
A few strands of saffron
Fresh mint leaves and
   roasted cashews for
   garnish

This dish sounds complicated to make but really isn't. The few extra steps and the few extra minutes will create a lovely, comforting pulao that is sure to become a favorite!

. . . .

1. Soak the morels in hot water until soft, about 30 minutes. Soak the cashews separately in hot water for 30 minutes as well.

2. Drain both and set aside. (You can save the mushroom stock for another use later, if you like.)

3. In a blender, grind the cashews to a paste; you can add up to 2 tablespoons water to help with the grinding process. Set aside.

4. Wash the morels in fresh water until no grit remains in them. Dry them well.

5. Mix the paneer, mint, and ⅛ teaspoon salt. Stuff into the morels. The stuffing should fill the mushroom but not fall out. Set aside.

6. In a deep saucepan, heat the vegetable oil over medium heat. Add the cardamom pod, bay leaf, cinnamon stick, and the onion.

7. Cook, stirring constantly, over medium-high heat until the onion begins to brown. This will take about 7 minutes.

8. Reduce the heat to medium. Add the cashew paste and cook for another 2 minutes, until the paste begins to change color. Add ½ teaspoon salt, the chile flakes, and the saffron and mix well. Add 1 cup of the chicken stock and bring to a boil. Add the morels. Cover and cook over medium-low heat for 10 minutes.

9. Add the rice and the remaining 1¾ cups of the stock. Bring to a boil.

10. Reduce the heat to low and cover. Cook for 15 to 20 minutes, until the rice is completely cooked and the moisture is all absorbed. If the rice seems moist at this point, increase the heat to medium-high and cook, stirring constantly, for a minute or so. The rice will remain just a bit moist but should not be clumpy at all.

11. Remove the cover and fluff with a fork. Serve garnished with fresh mint leaves and cashews.

We were in the heat of negotiation. Things were getting down to nickles and dimes. She was good at this, I could tell. She had done it many times before.

"I get more money from Dr. Gupta's wife and also the German friend of yours who sent you to me. You will need to increase your offer."

"Well, I guess I can. So, my final word: I will need twenty each week, on time and freshly prepared."

Beaming at me, she knew she had won and she agreed.

For delivery, we would meet halfway, in the Target parking lot. She did not mind taking a check but really for this, she would prefer cash. Fine. I could do cash.

I called my sister to tell her I had found a supplier. "Oh, you are lucky. There are no such people here; I have to go and get the commercial stuff."

Word spread locally and I had to share the name of the supplier with friends. Soon, she became so busy that I was having trouble getting my own supplies. "Why did you share

her name?" A smart, in-the-know buddy chided me, "you don't share these things, these are things that you only keep to yourself." Good advice, though too late.

All this took place ten years ago in Cleveland.

When I moved to Washington, D.C., I began a fresh search. I found her. A life-saver. She was older, more experienced, and able to supply a better product. She used the best to make the best. I was impressed. One taste and the family was hooked. "Now, don't tell everyone on the planet about her," my husband reminded me, forcing me to withdraw an idea I had for an article on her for a local publication. "Yes, she is all mine this time."

Yes, it is that sinister: finding and keeping a lady to make fresh *chapatis* for us. Chapatis, also known as *phuklas* or *rotis*, are Indian griddle breads that are a part of every meal. We use them as implements to scoop up curries. And for the record, I don't like making them at home. While I love the homemade taste, and preparing the dough and then making the bread isn't hard, it is time-consuming. With a newborn, two book deadlines, an eight-year-old with his projects, article deadlines, and everything else, making chapatis takes a back seat. Before you think less of me, let me tell you I am not the only one. I have dined at the homes of chefs, cookbook authors, celebrities, and many Indian friends and family who in India had a cook to make them but now use the services of a hard-to-find chapati lady—or use whole-wheat tortillas from Costco! There are of course many Indian Americans who make chapatis at home and if I happen to run into any of them, I befriend them immediately—I do love the taste of fresh homemade chapatis and will give in once in a while and make them from scratch.

Now, there are many of us who understand the problem of sourcing chapatis. A woman in Belgium who had read a few comments I had made on the subject contacted me by e-mail and said, "Please do a piece on that. We have one here. She does all our chapatis for the week and it is wonderful."

You can equate it to someone who could make you a great French loaf for dinner each week or someone who would make your pizza dough or your *injera,* an Ethiopian bread. I know there are those who consider it illegitimate, perhaps even sacrilegious to get someone else to make a staple for them. Thankfully, I am not one of those people!

My mother-in-law in Mumbai has a chapati lady; my mother in Delhi does; my sister in Arizona does; my sister-in-law does; my husband's aunt in Maryland does; and my friend Vrinda in New York now does. The list goes on and on. They all do it and all admit it. There are many others who do it but won't admit it.

I am not ashamed. In fact, as a food writer and cookbook author I love to cook but I love to cook things that I find interesting. Making chapatis is, to me, time-consuming and a bit of a messy proposition. I would rather spend my time making curries and pulaos and matching them with cocktails. I hold my head high as I call my chapati lady each week for my weekly dose.

Yes, the chapati lady is a critical

part of the Indian food chain in any major U.S. metropolitan area. They are housewives who make extra money on the side by making chapatis, savories like samosas, stuffed breads, and sometimes even curries. They usually don't drive, so pick-ups have to be arranged. But the product is wonderful: homemade whole-wheat rotis that aren't dry. Perfectly wrapped in plastic wrap and then foil, they stay fresh for up to two weeks.

These days, you can find fairly good chapatis at the local Indian grocer. In fact, in Vienna, Virginia, the grocer sells locally hand-made chapatis that always sell out before the week is over. Whole-wheat flour tortillas work well, too. They are what I have on stock in the fridge for emergencies, like when my chapati lady is out of town or when she is so busy that I need to find a new one! ☀

My Windex: Indian Basil

Do you remember the cure-all Windex in the movie *My Big Fat Greek Wedding*? In our house more than two decades ago, it was not Windex—it was basil. My grandmother swore by it with religious fervor. According to her, basil—holy basil or *tulsi* as it's known in Northern India—could cure anything. Have a cold or a tummy ache? Try basil tea. Have a headache? Smell the basil. Malaria? Poisoning? Heart disease? No problem: Basil in one of its many configurations can cure it.

True, basil is actually known in Ayurvedic medicine to be an elixir and does have legendary curative properties, but in our house it was a cure for *everything*: a broken heart, settling your mind/stomach/ears, even unemployment. All could be cured by a cup of basil tea.

In North Indian Hindu homes, many worship this plant, which is deemed to be the reincarnation of a divine goddess. In my grandmother's house, we feared it, or at least what she was able to conjure up with it. It all seemed relatively innocuous and harmless to the unsuspecting relatives who came over. They would come to socialize with her. They would begin with their plight of the day—someone missed the bus, another had a long wait for food in the ration line, others were simply complaining about the heat. We learned to tell if she liked them by what she offered them to drink. If she merely said to the servant to get a *thanda* (cold drink) they were not on her favorite list. But if they were offered the revered tulsi tea, we knew these people were dear to her heart. "*Pee lo, sab teek ho jayega,*" drink it, she would say, and all will be well. They would sit and talk endlessly over the cups of tulsi tea, or sorrow tea as I called it. They would drink it, thank her, and leave as if magically cured of what had ailed them.

She had few rules for us but one was to stay away from the tulsi, which we could never seem to do. It was at such a perfect short height for little fingers to pluck and eat the leaves. Her eagle eye, the one in the back of her head, would find out and we would be in trouble for the day. She cared for it a great deal, although as is customary in many parts of India, I never did see her pray to it.

After my grandparents died, their house was cleared out and locked up. A few years ago on a visit to Delhi, my father and I decided to visit this old house. It had clearly suffered the ravages of time. On a muggy day in Delhi, we stepped into the courtyard of this uninhabited home. Our steps left imprints in the dust as if we had disturbed the silence of history. I looked around, desperate for something familiar other than the walls and doors. And there it was: dried-up, shriveled, and wasted, yet still fixed in an old terra-cotta planter . . . my grandmother's tulsi. I could almost hear the ghosts in the background as the dried leaves rustled about. ✳

TOMATO-BASIL PILAF

 love basil in all its forms. I frequently add it to my rice, something I never saw my grandmother do. It adds a wonderful fresh flavor to this tomato pilaf, bringing out the tanginess of the tomatoes and the nutty flavor of the basmati. Indian basil is very hard to find in the United States, so I use either Italian basil or Thai basil.

. . . .

1. In a deep lidded saucepan, heat the vegetable oil over medium heat. Add the garlic, tomatoes, dried basil, and salt. Cook uncovered, stirring frequently, until the tomatoes are slightly softened, 4 to 5 minutes.

2. Add the rice and mix well. Add the broth and bring to a boil.

3. Reduce the heat to low. Cover and cook until the rice is tender, 18 to 20 minutes. Do not lift the cover while the rice is cooking.

4. Remove from the heat. Remove the large garlic pieces.

5. Serve hot, topped with fresh basil.

SERVES *4*

PREP/COOK TIME:

30 minutes

1 tablespoon vegetable oil

2 garlic cloves, lightly crushed

2 small tomatoes, diced

1½ teaspoons dried basil

¼ teaspoon table salt

1 cup white basmati rice

2 cups vegetable broth or water

Fresh basil leaves for garnish

CURRY LEAF BREAD

MAKES *one 1-pound Loaf*
PREP TIME: *15 minutes
hands on, 2 hours unattended.*
COOK TIME: *About 50
minutes*

4 cups all-purpose flour
2 tablespoons sugar
1 envelope (2¼
    teaspoons) quick-
    rising yeast
1 teaspoon table salt
1 teaspoon ground
    turmeric
1 teaspoon cumin seeds,
    crushed
2 tablespoons finely
    chopped fresh curry
    leaves (see Note)
2 tablespoons unsalted
    butter
¾ cup water (more if
    needed)
½ cup evaporated milk

I studied engineering in Bangalore well over fifteen years ago. I loved the city with its gardens and cool temperatures and open walking areas. I visited a few years ago and was sadly disappointed. The city I loved had become overrun with crowds and the light, open feeling was gone. But I did find that the food was still as fantastic as ever—and I made a new discovery. Local bakeries were baking up rolls flavored with Indian spices and herbs. Here is my rendition of curry leaf bread.

Since flours vary in their protein content from brand to brand and region to region, you might need to adjust the amount of liquid in this recipe.

. . . .

1. In a large bowl, whisk together the flour, sugar, yeast, salt, turmeric, cumin, and curry leaves.

2. Heat the butter, water, and evaporated milk just until the butter melts. Allow to cool until warm to the touch (110° to 120°F).

3. Gradually add the warm liquid to the dry ingredients and mix with a wooden spoon until a soft but not sticky dough forms. You may not need all of the liquid; but if the dough is too dry, add warm water a tablespoon at a time, until you get a soft dough.

4. Turn the dough out onto a clean floured work surface and knead for about 5 minutes, until you have a soft, smooth, and elastic dough.

5. Transfer the dough to a lightly greased bowl, cover with a damp towel, and allow to rise in a warm, draft-free place until doubled in bulk, 45 to 60 minutes.

6. Place the dough on a clean work surface and knead for a minute or two.

7. Shape and place in a greased 8½- by 4½-inch loaf pan, cover with a damp cloth, and allow to rise until dough is about 1 inch above top of pan, 45 to 60 minutes.

8. Meanwhile, preheat the oven to 375°F with a rack in the middle position.

9. Bake for 35 to 45 minutes or until the top is golden brown and the loaf sounds hollow when tapped on the bottom.

10. Remove from pan; cool on wire rack.

Note: Once and for all: curry leaves have nothing to do with curry powder! Curry powder, an invention of the British, is a collection of many spices (coriander, cumin, and others) but has no curry leaves. Curry leaves, actually *kari patta,* are native to South India. They are small, shiny, and very aromatic. Unlike bay leaves, these leaves can be eaten. I have not found anything that matches their lemony flavor and heady aroma. In desperation, lemon juice may be a substitute; it adds a tang but the taste does not match. There is a curry plant available in the United States that should not be mistaken for curry leaves. *Helichrysum italicum* does not taste even remotely like curry leaves. Buy curry leaves fresh when you need them. Tear the leaves off the stem and use as indicated in the recipe.

SUNDAY NIGHT SKILLET CHICKEN AND RICE

This is the dish to make when you are craving a hearty, comforting dish that has just the right warming spices. The best part? It takes very little time and can be cooking as you savor a glass of wine before dinner!

. . . .

1. In a large, deep lidded skillet, heat the oil over medium heat. Add the cinnamon stick and bay leaves. When the spices begin to sizzle, add the onion and ginger-garlic paste. Sauté for 5 to 7 minutes, until the onion begins to change color and soften.

2. Add the tomatoes and cook for 10 to 12 minutes, until the tomatoes are soft and the oil begins to separate from the sides of the mixture. You can use a potato masher to mash the tomatoes as they cook. If the mixture begins to stick to the sides of the skillet, add up to ¼ cup water.

3. Add the chile powder, turmeric, coriander, and salt to taste. Cook, stirring constantly for another minute.

4. Add the chicken and cook for 10 minutes, stirring constantly, until the chicken is brown on all sides and almost completely cooked through.

5. Add the rice and water and bring to a rolling boil.

6. Reduce the heat, cover, and cook for about 20 minutes on low heat, until the water is completely absorbed. The final dish will be barely moist.

7. Fluff the rice with a fork and serve.

DESSERTS

. . . .

There is only one way to describe traditional Indian desserts: very, very sweet. It is hard for me to convince non-Indians to try them, since they generally don't have the ultra-sweet tooth of most Indians! Many of these traditional desserts are milk-based and cooked with ghee (clarified butter), and lots (and lots and lots) of sugar.

I remember having a rather spirited discussion with Indian superstar Chef Sanjeev Kapoor on the eating habits of modern Indians and how things have changed over the years. Our discussion turned to desserts, as eating sweets is just as big with Indians as eating curries—perhaps even a bigger obsession. I was quoting study after study that proved such overly sweet desserts lead to weight gain, hypertension, etc. "Are Indians really turning toward healthier eating and exercise?" I asked. "Yes, of course, they are. Haven't you heard what is going on in your native Delhi?" he asked. The twinkle in his eye should have given it away, but I did not think anything of it at the time and took the bait. "No, what is happening in Delhi?" (Delhi is known for being over the top in terms of people spending money on anything and everything.) "Ah," he smiled, "people in Delhi are taking exercise very seriously. In fact, the rich people have hired servants to go walk for them every morning!"

Here are some modern Indian desserts that are robust in flavor but lower in sugar and ghee than traditional Indian sweets. These desserts are easy to make and really play up the ingredients and style of Indian cooking.

EXOTIC FRUIT SALAD

The sweetness of the lychees, papaya, and mango makes this a perfect way to end a heavy meal. Although persimmon is not an Indian fruit; when it is in season, I always add it to this dish, as it complements the flavor very well. If you cannot find fresh lychees, canned lychees are just fine. You can also use ½ cup of the Pomegranate Chutney (page 43) instead of the guava nectar.

. . . .

Toss all the ingredients in a nonreactive bowl until well combined. Chill, covered, for 30 minutes. Serve garnished with mint sprigs.

Did you know . . . lychees do not ripen after picking, so when you shop for them look for the ones that are the most fragrant. They have a very bumpy outer skin that is bright red when they are ripe. Crack open the skin and discard. Eat the pulpy fruit and throw away the single pit.

SERVES *4*

PREP TIME: *10 minutes, plus 30 minutes to chill*

1 cup peeled, seeded, and halved lychees (about 8 to 10 lychees)

1½ cups papaya chunks (about ½ medium papaya)

1½ cups mango chunks (about 1½ medium mangoes)

¼ cup guava nectar or juice

2 tablespoons minced fresh mint or up to 1 teaspoon dried mint

Mint sprigs for garnish

STRAWBERRY AND KIWI PUDDING

SERVES *4*

PREP TIME: *10 minutes,
plus 30 minutes to chill*

2 cups full-fat or 2% fat
Greek-style yogurt

1 cup sliced strawberries,
pureed

1 cup finely chopped
peeled kiwis (about 2
kiwis)

¼ cup liquid honey (or
more to taste)

8 teaspoons superfine
sugar to caramelize
(optional)

Sliced strawberries and
kiwis for garnish
(optional)

This very traditional Indian dessert, *shrikhand,* is generally made with either plain yogurt and sugar or yogurt flavored with saffron and mango. One of my American friends adapted my traditional shrikhand recipe with the wonderful and charming flavors of strawberry, and I embellished it with a touch of kiwi.

Traditionally this dessert uses yogurt that is wrapped in cloth and allowed to drain to release all the whey. But to save time, use Greek-style yogurt, which is already thick and creamy.

. . . .

1. Place the yogurt, strawberry puree, kiwis, and honey in a bowl and use a spatula to combine them.

2. Adjust the honey; if the strawberries are underripe, you will need more honey.

3. Divide the dessert into four attractive bowls.

4. Chill for about 30 minutes.

5. If you are going to caramelize, evenly sprinkle 2 teaspoons sugar on top of the yogurt mixture in each bowl. Light your brûlée torch and move the flame close to the sugar until it begins to melt. Now move the flame in small circles over the sugar until it begins to brown. Wait for about 5 minutes and then serve.

6. If you're not going to caramelize, garnish with additional sliced strawberries and kiwis and serve.

Note: As a variation sometimes I top this dessert with super-fine sugar that I then caramelize. It is a trick I learned from Chef K. N. Vinod of Indique in Washington, D.C. Try this only if you own a brûlée torch. (Even very hot broilers start to cook the yogurt while the sugar is browning and we don't want that!) Use superfine sugar as it caramelizes quickly and gives a thin, sweet crust to the dessert. If you don't have a torch, try making some caramel shards: Heat some sugar and water together without stirring until it turns a lovely amber color. Remove from heat and pour it onto a rimmed cookie sheet lined with parchment paper. Allow to cool. Break into shards and stick them into the pudding immediately before serving. You can also top the pudding with candied pistachios, candied pecans, or candied almonds.

SAFFRON-CARDAMOM MACAROONS

MAKES *35 to 38 small macaroons*

PREP/COOK TIME:
30 minutes, plus 30 minutes to cool

Nonstick cooking spray
One 14-ounce package shredded sweetened coconut
10 ounces sweetened condensed milk such as Eagle brand, from a 14-ounce can
1½ teaspoons ground cardamom
1 teaspoon saffron threads, crushed
¼ teaspoon table salt
2 small egg whites, whipped to peaks (see Notes)

Macaroons are a personal favorite. I have added cardamom, a flavor I love. You can also try these with mild curry powder (add ¼ teaspoon), ground cinnamon (½ teaspoon), or—well, you get the idea! There are no limits, only flavorful macaroons waiting to be tried. These can be stored at room temperature or in the refrigerator.

. . . .

1. Heat the oven to 350°F. Prepare a baking sheet by lining it with parchment paper and lightly spraying with nonstick spray.

2. Combine the coconut, condensed milk, cardamom, saffron, and salt in a bowl. (It will form a mixture that is not like typical cookie dough, but once the egg whites are folded in, the mixture will hold together.)

3. Gently fold in the whipped egg whites.

4. Using a spoon, mold the mixture into tablespoon-size balls and place 1 inch apart on the prepared pan.

5. Bake the macaroons for 14 to 16 minutes, until the exterior is very slightly brown, the middle is still soft, and the bottoms are beginning to turn golden brown.

6. Remove from the oven. Allow to cool for about 20 minutes.

7. Serve at room temperature. These can be stored in an airtight container for up to a week.

Notes: Don't use wax paper when baking; it will smoke in the oven. Parchment paper works best.

Use room-temperature eggs. I like to add a touch of lemon juice, salt, or cream of tartar to help the eggs get to the peaks. Once you begin to whisk them and they reach the soft peak stage, *stop*. If you continue to beat them, the proteins will break down and you will have a soft mess on your hands.

LYCHEE PHIRNI

SERVES *4*

PREP/COOK TIME:
45 minutes, including cooling

2½ cups whole milk

1 cup heavy cream

2 whole star anise

6 tablespoons rice flour

¼ cup sugar

One 20-ounce can whole,
   pitted lychees, drained
   and roughly pureed
   (leave in a few chunks
   of lychees)

Fresh sliced lychees and
   whole star anise for
   garnish

In its most traditional form, this dessert is made by soaking basmati rice in water, grinding it, and squeezing out the liquid before cooking it with milk and sugar. Here is an Indian-inspired variation made with lychee puree. You can use canned lychees for this. Taste the pudding before adding the lychee—you may need to add additional sugar depending on the sweetness of the lychees. For a variation of flavor, add about 2 or 3 cardamom pods instead of the star anise.

. . . .

1. In a deep, heavy-bottomed lidded saucepan, combine 2 cups of the milk and the heavy cream. Add the star anise. Bring to a boil over medium-high heat, stirring frequently to prevent burning. Boil about 2 to 3 minutes, then reduce the heat to medium-low. Remove the star anise and discard.

2. Dissolve the rice flour in the remaining ½ cup milk. Add this and the sugar to the hot milk and cook covered for about 15 minutes, until the mixture reaches a creamy consistency. Remove the cover 2 or 3 times during the cooking process to stir. Watch carefully: If the mixture begins to stick to the side, reduce the heat to low and continue to cook.

3. Remove from the heat. Allow to cool to room temperature.

4. Add the lychee puree and mix well.

5. Serve hot or cold, garnished with the sliced lychees and star anise.

The Soulful Granita

Shaved ice desserts are common on the streets of India. This is a bit different, both in terms of flavors and presentation. Rooh Afza, which translates to "that which nurtures the soul," is a popular syrup for making drinks and can be found in any Indian grocery store. If you are not serving this to children, add a touch of vodka for an extra zing. Rooh Afza is very sweet and does not require any additional sugar. I like the contrast of the lemon in this dish.

. . . .

1. Combine the Rooh Afza, lemon juice, and water in a saucepan and mix well to completely dissolve the syrup. Bring to a gentle boil, then remove from heat immediately and allow to cool.

2. If you are adding the vodka, do so now.

3. Pour the mixture into a wide, shallow pan and put it in the freezer.

4. Once the mixture begins to form ice crystals, stir it with a fork and repeat the stirring every hour. It will take about six hours to set.

5. When ready to serve, use a fork to break up the ice crystals and spoon into attractive glasses or cups. Garnish with a fresh mint leaf.

SERVES 6

PREP/COOK TIME:
20 minutes plus 6 hours to freeze

6 tablespoons Rooh Afza
2 tablespoons fresh lemon juice
3 cups water
¼ cup vodka (optional)
Fresh mint leaves for garnish

Mango and Champagne Granita

Serves *6*

Prep/Cook time:
20 minutes plus 6 hours to freeze

One 1-pound 14-ounce
    can or two 15-ounce
    cans mango slices such
    as Ratna Mango slices,
    drained and pureed
2 tablespoons liquid
    honey
⅛ teaspoon saffron
    threads, crushed
2 tablespoons sweetened
    lime juice such as
    Rose's
½ cup Champagne or
    sparkling wine
Saffron threads for
    garnish

I make this frequently even when mangoes are not in season. If you find fresh Alphonso mangoes, now legal in the United States, this dessert will triple in flavor! Be sure to adjust the amount of honey used, as the Alphonso fruit tends to be extremely sweet.

. . . .

1. Puree the mangoes, honey, crushed saffron, lime juice, and Champagne in a blender until smooth.

2. Pour the mixture into a wide, shallow pan and freeze.

3. Once the mixture begins to form ice crystals, stir it with a fork and repeat the stirring every hour. It will take about 6 hours to set.

4. When ready to serve, use a fork to break up the ice crystals and spoon into attractive glasses or cups.

5. Serve garnished with a strand or two of saffron.

Did you know . . . the legendary poet Mirza Ghalib was an ardent lover of mangoes and is said to have tasted many of the thousands of varieties of mangoes found in India. He is noted as saying, "In my opinion, there are only two necessary requirements concerning mangoes. Firstly, they should be sweet and secondly, they should be plentiful."

Bowls of Blessings, Bowls of Bliss

BB guns and transvestite nuns on TV shows define my first memory of my very first week in the United States. The United States, specifically Lynchburg, Virginia, was nothing like I had imagined it. Growing up in the Middle East in the early eighties, my only exposure to America was through a government-controlled TV station that showed the saintly *Cosby* show and the spotless *Facts of Life*. We did rent movies, so I had expectations of tall buildings and cops dressed like Don Johnson running around saving gorgeous women. Lynchburg, however, was nothing like I had imagined. In the middle of the Bible Belt, its claim to fame was Jerry Falwell and Liberty University. A small town, it almost seemed lost in time—untouched by the modern world. I had imagined, perhaps naively, wealth, prosperity, abundance, and yes, a few very good looking cops.

Huddled in a small room in Lynchburg, I watched Jerry Springer and cried as I heard college kids shoot bottles in the backyard of my rented house. If I am honest, even worse than the difference in culture was the fact that I was lonely. Painfully introverted at the time, I had made no friends. People were friendly but at a distance. I could find no companion; I was miserable and alone. I remember spending several nights curled up on the floor with a picture of Lord Krishna in my hands, crying and begging for help. I was quietly unhappy in India with my engineering degree; why did I come here to be miserable again? The tears flowed. Leaving Virginia and going back was not an option. The Gulf War had just broken out. My father, back home in Bahrain where I grew up, was beyond anxious. I had to stay put.

I needed comfort, I needed home. And there was only one way I knew how. I was going to cook.

I had no car and no way of finding a local Indian store, if indeed there was one in this small town. Instead, I found a kind family on campus who happily lent me some cardamom and basmati rice.

I began to make rice pudding.

I poured the startlingly white milk into a deep pan, and brought it to a boil, never taking my eyes off the pot. I know what they say about a watched pot not boiling, but it was almost as though I were watching to see if someone would magically come out of my pot to save me from the loneliness that had taken over every inch of my being. I crushed the cardamom and added sinfully excessive amounts of sugar. And then the rice. I sat at the kitchen counter, in my rented shared college home, and wept. The rice would not cook fast enough. The cardamom would not give off its characteristic aroma. The milk would not release its cream. Nothing was working. My mother called as I picked up the pot to throw the contents into the sink. I put the pot back and retreated to my room with the phone. The call lasted thirty minutes. As I hung up the phone, I heard my kind roommate call from the kitchen, "What are you making? It smells absolutely divine in here."

I rushed out to see the milk and rice in perfect unison. The cardamom had taken over the air in the room. The pudding, thick and creamy, was at a perfect simmer. My roommate took a spoonful. "Wow, it's sweet but it's good. Is it like a rice pudding of some sort?"

Before I could answer, my only friend on campus walked in the door. Sameer, who had also come to the United States to study, was the first person I had met on campus. I had called him earlier to tell him about the shooting. "Are you okay? Those kids were just playing around, it really is nothing to worry about." He smiled his cherubic smile. "I did not know you could cook. What is that you are making?"

That was the first taste he ever had of my cooking; we have now been married fifteen years. (My mother-in-law was shocked when I made rice pudding to welcome them on their visit from India to our new home in the United States. Later she told me that in their part of India, rice pudding is prepared during periods of mourning. I had no idea!)

Rice pudding has always been my favorite dish. I don't really view it as a dessert. I can eat it for breakfast, lunch, dinner, and tea. I am known to serve it at random times of the day. My family obliges these idio-syncrasies, thankfully. Indian rice pudding is very different from traditional American rice pudding which is baked in the oven for long hours.

After leaving Lynchburg and spending a year studying in Washington, D.C., in 1992 I moved to Cleveland, Ohio where I met my closest friend Sandy. A spitting image of Fran Drescher (minus the accent), Sandy was everything I ever wanted in a friend—kind, funny, with an insatiable appetite for life and food. We spent many lunch hours together; we worked in the same building at the time and our favorite place to have lunch was a tiny joint in a dilapidated old building that served Indian curries and Greek rice pudding topped with ground cinnamon. We would spend our precious hour at lunch devouring the rice pudding after pretending to eat the obligatory curry that accompanied it, and we would talk—about her difficult time with her personal relationships, my own hard time making peace with a professional career that I neither cared for nor wanted. Nothing could dissuade us from our pudding afternoons, not even the miserable Cleve-

land snow or the incessant traveling I had to do for my job.

I requested her to be my first-born's god-aunt, a role she took very seriously. When my first son was born, I could not wait for him to start eating. Annaprasaran is a ritual in which Hindus give the first bite of *anna* (rice) to their children. Jai's first bite, after pureed peas, was a tiny bit of rice pudding which he promptly spit out. Of course, as the years progressed, he developed the same love for it that his parents have.

Even after I left Cleveland, Sandy and I stayed in touch. Our friendship endured marriages, lay-offs, babies, miscarriages, transfers, new cities, and new friends. It grew stronger and stronger. We often joked on the phone that we needed to get together to eat rice pudding again; it felt like a betrayal to eat it alone. Clearly she missed our afternoons as much as I did.

Then one day several months after leaving Cleveland, I picked up the phone to call her. I had just been diagnosed with a medical issue and wanted a shoulder to cry on. "Damn it," I told her, "I have so much work to do and this asinine thing is keeping me from it. I have to be on bed rest, and I can't do anything I want." She listened patiently, reminding me about all that was good in my life. But I would not listen. I complained and she listened, offering humor and calm to soothe my nerves.

"How have *you* been?" I asked off-handedly. When you have been friends with someone for fifteen years, the obvious never seems important enough to be asked.

She was quiet. Oh no, I thought, something is wrong with her dad. He had been ill, or maybe it's her sister.

"I got diagnosed with cancer the month you left," she said simply. "I have lost all my hair, have had chemotherapy, and am now waiting to see if it is all gone or still there."

Gorgeous at forty-one, with two small kids, a great career, a husband who loves her, my friend is the epitome of the American dream. In her pain, she still found the time to listen to my now not-so-critical issues.

We talked and cried together for a few hours on the phone. I guess what is important and what is not changes at a moment's notice. "I want to grow old together," she said, "we do have that option, don't we."

I went to visit her. I did not recognize the woman who answered the door. She looked like a ghost of her former self. I sat down and began to talk to her, averting my eyes so she could not see my tears. Then I looked up and looked in her eyes. I saw my friend. I saw a resolve to live. To beat her illness.

After I left her and flew home, I made a vow. I used to write sonnets on rice pudding——an evening with rice pudding meant definite celebration and soul-stirring elation.

I vowed never to eat it again until my one wish was granted.

I was determined to fight back in some way, any way. People fast all the time. They fast to pray and ask for wishes. I have never been good at either. I am a clumsy devotee at best. I had never needed to make a deal with God before, but this time was different. I was praying. I was determined. I was begging. He had to listen to me—she had to get well. People give up food for Lent all the time, right? I could do this . . .

When she recovered, I decided, I could make a bowl of rice pudding and feast on it to celebrate all that is right about life.

I wrote about rice pudding during my vow. Several times. Yet I could not get myself to even look at a bowl of it without weeping. My logical self knew that my not eating a dish could in no way help a friend who was ill. How could my giving up something I loved help her fight a life-threatening illness? Love, devotion, and hope reside somewhere beyond intellect and logic. I don't know if my prayers and my vow helped. I don't particularly care to know. I do know that they helped me deal with a situation that was breaking my heart and threatening to break my soul and my spirit. The love of a dish between friends kept me praying and begging for mercy and more. I never told her about my vow. I never told anyone. It did not matter. All that mattered was that she got well.

You are seeing a recipe here today because my friend beat her enemy.

My rice pudding sonnets are coming back to sing about bringing me the love of my life, my husband, and a true-once-in-a-lifetime friend. ❊

Rice Pudding and Mango Parfait

Serves 6

Prep/Cook time: *1½ hours, mostly unattended, plus 1 hour to chill*

3 cups whole milk

2 to 4 tablespoons sweetened condensed milk (see Note)

¼ cup white basmati rice, rinsed and drained

1 teaspoon cardamom seeds, crushed

1 ripe mango, peeled and diced

This dish is not only tasty (of course!) but has a very striking presentation. I have served it at many dinner parties just after guests have announced, "I could not eat another bite of anything. I am so full." And then they have proceeded to polish off this entire dessert!

This recipe uses cardamom seeds. To obtain them, open a green cardamom pod and use your fingers to coax the tiny seeds out. Pound them gently using a mortar and pestle or put them in a heavy-duty plastic bag and pound them with a hammer.

. . . .

1. In a deep saucepan, bring the whole milk and condensed milk to a boil over medium heat. Stir constantly to prevent scorching.

2. Reduce the heat to medium-low. Add the rice and cardamom and mix well. Continue to cook for about 50 minutes, until the milk has reduced by half and you obtain a creamy consistency. Stir frequently while cooking.

3. Remove from the heat and allow to come to room temperature.

4. Refrigerate, covered, for at least an hour.

5. When ready to serve, spoon some pudding into a wine glass, layer with some mango, and add another layer of rice pudding. Serve immediately.

Note: Use 4 tablespoons of condensed milk if you like your rice pudding really sweet. With 2 tablespoons, it is sweet but not overwhelmingly so.

$\mathcal{N}$ote: If you have a mango that is firm, peel it and then use a vegetable peeler to create thin mango slices. Arrange the slices on a plate and place a scoop of the rice pudding in the center of the mango "carpaccio."

$\mathcal{D}$id you know . . . green cardamom is used in various forms around the world: people brew it in coffee, add it to liquors and perfumes, sauté it with rice and meats, and in India it is eaten raw, whole (pod and seeds and all) as a digestive after a meal. It is also sold covered in *vark,* an edible silver foil, that makes it appear like a small shiny stone.

PINWHEELS OF PLEASURE

MAKES *12 cookies*

PREP/COOK TIME:
25 minutes

**A few tablespoons flour
for dusting**

**1 frozen puff pastry sheet
such as Pepperidge
Farm, thawed**

3 tablespoons honey

**¼ cup ground blanched
almonds**

**1 teaspoon fennel seeds,
roughly pounded (see
Note)**

I once interviewed the author of a coffee book who described the moment she tasted her first cup of "real coffee" as a "GodShot" moment, adding that "Hemingway was right—the first time, the earth does move." I feel that way about these cookies. These cookies are not very sweet, I feel, but just right. You can increase the honey a touch if you like sweeter cookies. Also, they taste best as soon as they are made.

To prepare the almonds, soak them in boiling water for about a minute and then drain. Allow to cool. Remove the skins of the almonds; they will slip off. Pat them dry and then grind them in a spice or coffee grinder to a coarse grind—not a fine grind, just a coarse grind without any large pieces of almonds. Their texture should be a little coarser than dried bread crumbs.

. . . .

1. Heat the oven to 450°F. Line a large cookie sheet with parchment paper. Lightly dust a clean work surface with flour.

2. Roll out the pastry sheet into a 10 x 12-inch rectangle on the work surface.

3. Drizzle the honey over the entire pastry sheet. Sprinkle the almonds over the sheet, then sprinkle the fennel over the sheet.

4. Now roll the pastry sheet into a pinwheel, forming a log.

5. Cut the log into 12 cookies. Place the cookies flat on the cookie sheet, about 1 inch apart. At this point, I find it helpful to refrigerate them for about half an hour or so before baking. I find it helps them hold their shape better.

6. Bake on the middle rack until you see the top of the cookies begin to brown, about 8 minutes. Flip over and bake for another 7 to 8 minutes.

7. Remove from the oven and allow to cool completely on the cookie sheet before serving.

Note: Why pound the fennel? This helps the fennel to release its flavor as it releases the oils stored inside the seed.

CHILLED MANGO-PAPAYA SOUP

SERVES 4

PREP TIME: *10 minutes plus 2 hours to chill*

1 medium papaya peeled, seeded, and roughly chopped (see Note)

1 mango, peeled, seeded and roughly chopped

½ cup unsweetened coconut milk

2 tablespoons golden rum (optional)

½ teaspoon table salt

1 tablespoon fresh lime juice

1 tablespoon crushed pineapple for garnish

Fresh mint leaves for garnish

I have a weakness for mangoes and papayas, and when they are in season, you can be assured that a bowl of this soup is in our fridge, almost all the time. It is such a simple dish, yet so flavorful and perfect for the hot summer months. If you cannot find fresh mango, you can use the canned slices. Just be sure to drain and then gently rinse them before use to remove any excess sweet syrup.

. . . .

1. In a blender or food processor, process the papaya and mango until smooth. Strain though a fine-mesh strainer into a large bowl. (Alternatively, you can leave a few small pieces of fruit in the soup for added texture.)

2. Whisk in the coconut milk, rum (if using), salt, and lime juice.

3. Cover and refrigerate for 2 hours or until well chilled.

4. To serve, adjust the seasonings to taste and pour the soup into chilled bowls. Garnish with crushed pineapple and mint leaves. (I frequently serve scoops of vanilla ice cream in the center of these soup bowls!)

Note: Picking a ripe papaya is an easy task: look for a golden-yellow skin on the outside and a fruit that yields to gentle pressure. The skin may have some discoloration but as long as it is not damaged, it is fine. Slice off the top and cut it lengthwise. Scoop out the seeds and then cut the fruit, discarding the skin. The skin tends to be very bitter so make sure you do take it all off.

Raspberry and Fig Jam Topping

$\mathcal{I}$n India, figs are often used to prepare desserts. I have always loved figs but the little things are notoriously seasonal. To indulge my cravings I developed a simple recipe that uses prepared fig spread along with other fruits to create a topping similar to a compote. You can add more water if you like your topping thinner.

. . . .

1. In a medium saucepan combine the fig jam, water, and star anise. Cook over low heat, stirring often, until the jam melts.

2. Add the cinnamon and black pepper. Add the strawberries and raspberries and cook for 3 to 4 minutes, over low heat, until the fruits are tender.

3. Remove from the heat and stir occasionally, until mixture cools to room temperature. Remove the star anise.

4. Serve as a topping for frozen yogurt, pound cake, or cheesecake. Refrigerate, covered, for up to a week.

MAKES *about 2 cups (3 servings of ½ cup each)*
PREP/COOK TIME: *about 20 minutes, plus time to cool*

½ cup fig jam such as Organic Adriatic Fig Spread
¼ cup water
1 whole star anise
Pinch of ground cinnamon
Pinch of freshly ground black pepper
¼ cup diced fresh strawberries
¼ cup chopped raspberries

GUAVA FOOL

SERVES *4*

PREP TIME: *5 minutes*

¼ cup chilled heavy
  cream
½ to ¾ cup pink guava
  puree, chilled (see
  Note)
Whipped cream for
  garnish

Mom always made mango fool for us, but there is nothing foolish about this delightful dessert. A fool is a dessert prepared with a fruit puree and cream. In my adaptation, guava puree is folded into whipped cream and served in tall glasses topped with—guess what?—yes, more whipped cream. If you are feeling adventurous, make a batch with guava and another batch with papaya. Layer them alternately in pretty wine glasses. Top with freshly whipped cream and serve immediately. The key to making this is not to mix but to fold the puree and the cream so that you can see streaks of each; if you mix it, it will look like a light pink cream. The taste won't change, of course, but the presentation will.

Use the best purees you can find. I like the ones available from L'Epicerie (www.lepicerie.com). They sell a pink guava puree that is best used in this recipe and other recipes in the book that call for guava puree. If you find guavas that are still creamy white inside, you cannot use them here as they will be too tart. Slice them, sprinkle on lemon juice and chaat masala, and enjoy the snack, and then go out and look for guavas that are pink inside, like the Patillo or Blitch varieties. You will have an easier time finding pink pulp which is sold at various online retailers or ethnic stores. By the way—the pink guava puree indicates the puree is pink, not the guava, which is yellowish-green on the outside!

. . . .

1. In a cold bowl with cold beaters, whip the heavy cream until it forms soft peaks.

2. Fold in the guava puree. Do this gently, using your spatula to gently fold the two. Do not blend. The idea is to keep the colors separate.

3. Divide evenly among four wine glasses.

4. Top with a touch of whipped cream. Serve immediately.

Note: If you can find fresh, ripe guavas, do use them for the puree. In India, the really ripe guavas are sweet and pink on the inside. They are very aromatic; the fruit should yield to gentle pressure. While the yellowish-green skin is edible, you will discard it to make the puree. After you puree the guavas, you can run the puree through a sieve to get a silkier puree. Many Korean and other ethnic stores sell guava puree so you don't have to do all the work.

GUAVA-COCONUT KULFI

SERVES *16 (¼ cup each)*

PREP TIME: *5 minutes hands-on, plus overnight to freeze*

1½ cups Cool Whip or
    whipped cream
One 14-ounce can
    sweetened condensed
    milk
1 cup unsweetened
    coconut milk
1½ cups pink guava puree
    (see page 246)
2 to 3 drops red food color

This easy, no-cook recipe for an Indian version of ice cream uses condensed milk and no eggs! You can play with the flavors; try pineapple puree instead of guava or even fig puree—it is delicious!

. . . .

Combine all the ingredients in a bowl and mix well. Pour into ice-cream molds or kulfi molds (available from Indian grocers). Cover and freeze overnight. Serve.

Renewing My Spirit

I had been on the go all day—son's haircut, soccer practice, grocery shopping, mall, post office, the never-ending cycle of responsible adulthood.

By eight o'clock, I was tired, hungry, and depressed. I wanted to crawl into bed with a glass of wine and whine. I wanted to forget about my grown-up life.

My husband reminded me that he was ready to take my son out so I could go to girls' night at a neighbor's house. I had completely forgotten about that—the neighbor had left a message earlier that week to "Come and join us as we celebrate being us."

I wanted to cancel.

I picked up the phone to make an excuse but then hung up. She had always been so kind to me and I thought it would be rude if I did not show up, at least for a few minutes. So I took the short stroll over to my neighbor's house.

The neighbor, an embassy wife whom I shall call Mina, is not a close friend, but I admire her spirit and inexplicable, constant optimism. Dark hair, olive skin, sparkling eyes, six kids, and nearing forty, she still looks better than most seventeen-year-olds I know. I don't know how she makes the time to do all she does and yet be so totally present in each moment. For instance, she does not customarily ask, "How are you?" and then walk away. She waits for an answer and then actually responds—she wants to know how you are, what you are doing, how your kids are feeling. Perhaps this is why I felt compelled to go to her party despite my exhaustion.

I dressed in a black pants suit and an orange silk shirt patterned with small maroon leaves. Casual, but hey, it was clean! When I entered her house I saw some women I had never met and a few more neighbors all dressed to the hilt—flowing gowns, glittering diamonds, perfectly coifed hairstyles, manicured nails, and for many of them, no customary veils. I felt like Cinderella before she got all dressed up for the ball.

As the guests trickled in, the room began to look like a meeting place for the United Nations. Wives of ambassadors from well-known countries, to nations whose names, I am ashamed to admit, I had never heard. The languages spoken were as different as the outfits the women wore. I began to feel distinctly uncomfortable. They were all so lovely and here I was, a harried woman just trying to get to the end of the day. I did not feel I was good enough to keep company with this group of perfect women. As I was thinking of leaving, Mina grabbed me to help her fix beverages in the kitchen.

I began to pour the drinks— pineapple juice, apple juice, sodas, and water. As I passed a drink to each guest, she would take a sip, then get up and kiss me on the cheek, introduce herself, and seem genuinely happy to meet me. The "spirits" were not in the glasses but around them in the form of these beautiful women with glowing skins and inquiring eyes.

When I put the serving tray down, they grasped me by the hand and invited me to sit with them.

One of them taught her native language at a U.S. government office; another was on the board of her school PTA. Their English was flawless. A few others who did not speak perfect English managed to convey their emotions better than most native English speakers. We discussed topics ranging from summer schools for kids to bad celebrity haircuts to the views of Rush Limbaugh. I began to realize as we talked that many were meeting each other for the first time. I wasn't the only stranger in the room.

Our host announced that dinner was served. It was a grand feast of chicken layered with rice, fried onions, and almonds, a yogurt dip laced with olive oil, and a fresh green salad. It was accompanied by an oven-baked layered bread dish drizzled with honey and warm butter. One guest had brought a large dish of sautéed lamb snuggled in a sauce of caramelized onions and tomatoes and topped with pan-fried slices of succulent eggplant. Yes, I did use succulent and eggplant in one sentence—whatever she had done to that eggplant, it competed with the lamb for taste and won.

If an outsider had walked in at this moment, it would have been hard to differentiate between the host and her guests——everyone was helping as if each were the host in her own home.

As I helped myself to a tempting pink salad made with beets, a woman who knew I was a food writer, began to tell me how she had prepared it. She then went on to explain the stories behind the other dishes. I was fascinated to learn that many of the women at the party used pressure cookers in their kitchens, as I do for Indian food. With most of my current friends, and even family, the very mention of a pressure cooker sends them into a tizzy with past memories of bad experiences (real or imagined). There was a connection here; we had found common ground.

As dinner progressed the laughter in the room vibrated with energy; a perfect chemistry had begun to develop.

Then Mina entered the room and said, "Now we dance."

Dance? I wondered who we were supposed to dance with. There were only women here. I thought back to my childhood. India has many customs that involve women getting together and dancing and singing but these activities usually surround an occasion like a wedding or the birth of a child. There was no occasion here. I sat next to an older neighbor, a blond-haired, porcelain-skinned, gentle South Carolina beauty who nudged me, saying, "This will be fun."

Rhythmic belly-dancing music began. One of the women got up and began to dance, gently swaying her hips to the music and then swiveling them as the beat got faster. She came over and took my hand and the hand of the Carolina beauty.

"We don't know how to do this," we pleaded with the dancer.

"You don't need to know anything," the dancer whispered. "Just close your eyes and let the music guide you."

I began to sway. I don't know how long I was dancing. When the song ended and another began, I opened my eyes. The room was filled with women gracefully dancing and moving to the music. I began to feel alive and to laugh out loud. The frustrations of my day were mere memories now. I was transported back home to the singing and dancing during traditional festivals and weddings, to the time when being together and celebrating was all that was important.

A young dancer pulled a scarf tagged with bells from her bag and tied it around her waist. The gracefulness of her movements seemed to be magnified by the scarf. I continued to dance, to learn the new music, to learn the beat. I began to let a totally new culture, a merging of so many cultures, enchant me and take over this night.

As we danced and danced, I knew I didn't want this night to end.

I approached Mina as she danced.

"I must leave," I said. "I must leave with this feeling of celebration. I must leave now so I will always want to come back." ❄

METRIC and OTHER EQUIVALENCIES

LIQUID EQUIVALENCIES

U.S.	METRIC
¼ teaspoon	1.25 milliliters
½ teaspoon	2.5 milliliters
1 teaspoon	5 milliliters
1 tablespoon	15 milliliters
1 fluid ounce	30 milliliters
¼ cup	60 milliliters
⅓ cup	80 milliliters
½ cup	120 milliliters
1 cup	240 milliliters
1 pint (2 cups)	480 milliliters
1 quart (4 cups)	960 milliliters (.96 liter)
1 gallon (4 quarts)	3.84 liters

DRY MEASURE EQUIVALENCIES

U.S.	METRIC
1 ounce (by weight)	28 grams
¼ pound (4 ounces)	114 grams

1 pound (16 ounces)	454 grams
2.2 pounds	1 kilogram (1,000 grams)

IMPERIAL MEASUREMENTS

Theoretically, both the United Kingdom and Canada use the metric system, but older recipes rely on the "imperial" measurement system, which differs from standard U.S. measurements in its liquid ("fluid") measurements:

U.S.	IMPERIAL
2.5 ounces	¼ cup
5 ounces	½ cup ("gill")
10 ounces	1 cup
20 ounces	1 pint
40 ounces	1 quart

INDEX

E

eggplant:
  pan-seared, with ginger
    and honey, 130
  and tomatoes with cilantro,
    131
eggs:
  beating, tips, 231
  curried salad with
    caramelized onion, 166
  masala omelet with green
    chile chutney, 78–79
eGullet.org, 137, 152
Egyptians, ancient, 107
emerald-ade, 58–59
exotic fruit salad, 227

F

feni (cashew nut liquor), 49
fennel:
  -and-coriander crusted
    lamb chops, 165
  -chile dry rub, 40
  paste, 185
  roasted cauliflower with,
    137
  -rubbed fish fillets, 185
fennel seeds, 26, 40
  pounding, 243
fenugreek, whole roast
  chicken with, 157
fenugreek leaves, dried, 26
fenugreek seeds, 26, 38

fig(s):
  date with, 92–93
  jam, and raspberry
    topping, 245
  and paneer pizza, 202–3
  ripeness of, 106
  roasted spicy, yogurt, 106
fish and shellfish, 173–94
  catfish tamarind curry, 192
  chile squid, 176
  crabby vermicelli, 188–89
  curried scallops, 178
  dry crab masala, 182
  fennel-rubbed fish fillets,
    185
  fish fry, 177
  ginger shrimp, 88
  hot, hotter, hottest shrimp,
    183
  Monica's tomato and
    coconut fish curry, 187
  pan-seared trout with
    mint-cilantro chutney,
    186
  pomegranate shrimp, 179
  saffron mussel stew, 193
  salmon with kumquat
    chutney, 184
  shrimp à la José with
    coconut dipping sauce,
    98–99
  shrimp in green-mango
    butter sauce, 194
  shrimp rice, 208–9
  stuffed butterfish, 180

  tamarind-glazed honey
    shrimp, 181
  tilapia curry with roasted
    spices, 190–91
"Food, Father, and Faith,"
  45–48
fool, guava, 246–47
fried fish, 177
Frugal Gourmet, 179
fruit(s):
  exotic, salad, 227
  purees, 62

G

garam masala, 26
  chicken, 86–87
garlic:
  fresh crushed, rice and
    black-eyed peas with,
    133
  -ginger paste, 18
  red chile, and basil
    chicken, 162
  smashed potatoes, 132
Garten, Ina, 163
Ghalib, Mirza, 234
ghee (clarified butter), 22
Gill, Manjit Singh, 151–52
ginger:
  and carrot soup, curried,
    with pan-fried paneer,
    116–17
  -garlic paste, 18
  and honey marinade, 42